J. Arthur Hoyles

PUNISHMENT
in the
BIBLE

220.8

EPWORTH PRESS

British Library Cataloguing in Publication Data

Hoyles, J. Arthur
Punishment in the Bible.
1. Punishment in the Bible
I. Title
220.8'3646   BS680.P7/

ISBN 0–7162–0425–8

First published 1986
by Epworth Press
Room 190, 1 Central Buildings
Westminster, London SW1H 9NR

Typeset by The Spartan Press Ltd
Lyminmgton, Hants
and printed in Great Britain by
Richard Clay (The Chaucer Press) plc
Bungay, Suffolk

Contents

Acknowledgments

The author takes full responsibility for the views expressed in this book, which is the result of a research project at the University of Sheffield, but acknowledges a debt of gratitude to: Professor John W. Rogerson of the University of Sheffield, Professor Henry McKeating of the University of Nottingham, and Dr A. Skevington Wood, Former Principal of Cliff College, near Sheffield.

Introduction

The attempt to discover what the Bible has to say on any particular subject is likely to be frustrating. If the student begins his search in the belief that he will find clear and final answers to the moral questions of the present day he will soon be disillusioned. There are so many different points of view in this motley collection of documents covering over a thousand years of human history that, instead of a simple dogmatic system, he will be faced with a catalogue of conundrums. His aim should be to reach tentative conclusions rather than cast-iron certainties.

If he belongs to a school of thought which believes in literal or verbal inspiration of the Bible he may argue that everything in the sacred pages is true and reliable. He will affirm that the Holy Spirit gave the words to the writers and will likewise give the reader power to understand them. If the sceptical critic discovers inconsistencies or contradictions he will find refuge in antinomies in the firm belief that truth is greater than logic. There are people who provide proof-texts, giving chapter and verse, cheerfully regarding them as valid even though they are contradicted in other texts.

This study assumes that reason is a God-given faculty which must be brought to bear upon Biblical exegesis and that various systems of belief and practice in the ancient world have to be critically examined in the light of modern knowledge acquired by other disciplines. We are dealing with probabilities rather than certainties. We shall not shirk the conflicts which occur in this daunting library, nor be content with over-simplifications.

There are glaring examples of brutality in the annals of Israelite history, which contradict the general image of a gracious and merciful God. Two examples may be given: the first is the cruel vengeance which Samuel inflicted on the king of the Amalekites when he hewed Agag in pieces before the Lord in Gilgal (I Sam. 15.33). The other is: 'Happy shall he be who takes your little ones and dashes them against the rock' (Ps. 137.9). One needs considerable heuristic ingenuity in order to reconcile such savagery with the joyful affirmation that the Lord is merciful and gracious, slow to anger and abounding in steadfast love (Ps. 103.8).

A familiar technique for achieving a measure of harmony from the discordant sounds was to speak of *progressive revelation*. This concept emerged round about the middle of the nineteenth century as a tool to assist the reader to explain the apparent contradictions encountered in the scriptures. Its appearance almost coincided with that of the theory of evolution. In essence it means that the history of mankind, and in particular that of the Israelites, was ordered by divine providence and showed definite progress in social and ethical standards. Crude and superstitious episodes fitted into the evolutionary process by which the will of God was unfolded to successive generations.

The alternative view, expressed by H. L. Mansell in 1858, was that if God commanded a person to do something immoral, it ceased to be immoral because God commanded it. Such commands may have been for one occasion only and not to establish universal principles of conduct. It was not for man to question why God in his wisdom issued such instructions.[1] By way of criticism the new school of thought replied that if all parts of the Bible had equal validity the sacred text had little guidance to offer to society today.

So the theory of progressive revelation guided the Bible student for a hundred years. Scholars like Wellhausen and Peake sought to date the various books of the Old Testament so that they illustrated theological and ethical development. They recognized various setbacks and reversions to primitive customs, but there was certainly change and improvement in political organization when a collection of wandering tribes became a nation, and there was theological transformation from polytheism to monotheism, while religious beliefs were greatly influenced by the thought forms of Persian and Greek thinkers in the post-exilic period.

Whether there was a progression in the realm of morals is now seriously called in question. The theory was largely based on the dating of certain passages in the Pentateuch. For example, the stories of the flood, the destruction of Sodom and Gomorrah and the practice of human sacrifice which Abraham renounced on Mount Moriah, which were thought to be among the early writings, are now suspected of being post-exilic. One of the objects of this research is to discover how far the concept of progressive revelation can be applied to the theory and practice of punishment as they are expounded in the Bible.

A major question has to do with the relation between the Old Testament and the New. The coming of Jesus was seen by the early Christians as providing a new and unique stage in the history of God's revelation of himself. The apostles and fathers of the church formulated the creeds on the declaration that Christ was 'very God of very God . . . being of one substance with the Father'. Does this mean that his teaching and example become the basis of Christian ethics for all time? Is there now no point in considering the ethical principles which applied before the incarnation?

There have been scholars who have given an affirmative answer to these pertinent questions. As early as the first century Paul saw the spirit of the gospel as set over against the law of Judaism. In the second century Marcion announced that he could not perceive in nature or in the Old Testament the same love that was in the gospel of Christ. He proceeded to reject the former, but then found he had to reject much of the latter as well. Since the Reformation the relation between the two testaments has taken the form of rival claims as between gospel and law. Lutheran ethics have tended to see justification by faith as the ground of moral life for the Christian, while the law is seen as a device to control the secular state. Calvin saw no contradiction between law and gospel, so that to him the Old Testament was not, as in Luther, the background against which the light of the gospel shone, it was a present light in its own right.

It is a mistake, however, to think of the Old Testament as providing a system of laws and penalties. Those who cite the Book of Genesis as an unambiguous demand that murderers be executed are in a dilemma when they also read that the death penalty is also prescribed for adultery, blasphemy and cursing one's parents. When the laws were coded they represented what the authorities of the day felt to be right in the sight of God. They were not timeless expressions of the unalterable divine will. They changed in accordance with deepening sensitivity in the sphere of morals. They did not come about by supernatural dictation, but as a consensus of what at the time seemed self-evidently right.

As Professor Rogerson wrote in 1982:

The Old Testament teaches us that God approves what moral sensitivity at its best holds to be right. A dynamic model is introduced by the idea of natural morality, altering in accordance with deepening moral sensitivity.[2]

Rogerson made another observation in the same article. He said that one supreme motivation for moral achievement in Israel was the 'imperative of redemption', which he explained as the revelation of divine mercy in the deliverance of his people from slavery in Egypt. Because God had redeemed this weak and insignificant band from oppression, not because of their merit but out of his own steadfast love, they were to be merciful to one another and care for the poor and the oppressed. With its emphasis on total dependence upon God and need of his grace the Old Testament approximates to the New and is of immense value for making moral judgments, even though one is delivered from the security of precisely defined rules.

It must be already clear that side by side with the hewing of Agag in pieces before the Lord and the dashing of children against the rocks there are in the Old Testament some beautiful approximations to the Christian gospel of divine grace. As Dr Henry McKeating has pointed out, when God made a covenant with Abraham there were no conditions attached. There were no rules which his descendants were required to keep. The covenant was offered purely from God's grace. The stories of Joseph enshrine some of the profoundest theological ideas of the Bible. He does not hold his brothers' wickedness against them. He took the form of a slave and became the archetype of the suffering servant of God. There is much in pre-Christian literature that falls short of what is morally acceptable to us, says McKeating, but this does not mean that we should discount the whole Old Testament.[3]

There is no unanimity regarding the justifiable use of punishment in the New Testament either. Jesus enjoined love of one's neighbour and repudiated vengeance, but so did Jewish law (Luke 10.27; Matt. 5.44; Lev. 19.18). Paul told the Romans that if their enemy was hungry they must feed him, but the words he used were taken directly from the Old Testament (Rom. 12.20; Prov. 25.21). There is much in the theological ethics of the gospel that requires the Jewish literature to make it intelligible. There are also some crude statements in the New Testament which are not far removed from the butchery of Agag by Samuel.

We must be prepared to find a confusion of theory and practice in the penology of the Bible. Just as in modern times there are many views about capital punishment and prison conditions, so in the Bible various individuals and groups expressed their opinions in the light of the theological presuppositions of their time. Reason has to be brought to bear on the conflicting evidence in order to reach a consensus in a democratic state. It should be remembered that our conclusions are tentative and may change from one generation to another. We should not expect all Christians to subscribe to one doctrine, but neither should we assume that the majority is always right.

One source of confusion, which seems unavoidable, is the lack of any clear distinction between various types of wrongdoing. We are accustomed to distinguish between crime and sin, the former being an infringement of state laws, the latter an offence against God. This distinction would have had little meaning until the tribes achieved nationhood. Some scholars even doubt whether 'criminal law' was recognized in Israel. There was hardly a clear distinction between moral, ceremonial and civil law. The term *offender* is intended in this study to cover wrongdoers at different levels. Similarly the term *punishment* is understood to apply to the use of the rod by a father within his family, various forms of penalty inflicted by judicial authorities in a given community, correctional techniques adopted by ecclesiastical hierarchies and natural disasters when understood as 'acts of God' in response to human wickedness.

Having taken heed of the warnings we begin the safari. The journey will take us through the books of the Bible, where we shall look for ancient treasures; obelisks marking high moments of divine revelation, monuments to man's inhumanity to man, mountains of exquisite delight, canyons of darkness and gloom, motorways where the going is easy, dirt tracks where little progress is possible. If at journey's end we have collected little in the way of permanent truth, it may be possible to say that we travelled hopefully.

PART ONE

PUNISHMENT IN THE
OLD TESTAMENT

1 PUNISHMENT AS VENGEANCE

Although a division of Old Testament literature into historical periods cannot be contemplated in the light of present day scholarship, it may be feasible to assemble the date according to the theological ideas which have influenced the theory and practice of punishment over the period of two thousand years covered by the literature available. It is important to recognize that this does not assume definite progress in the social and moral development of the Israelite people.

The theme of the Old Testament is religion. Whatever subject is being discussed, whether it is biology, anthropology or politics, it is considered in relation to God. It is not unreasonable, therefore, to study Hebrew penology in the light of the theological presuppositions to which it is related. Even when we study the religious motivation in punishment we can only speak of general tendencies, for there is no way of fitting theological development into an infallible chronological pattern.

According to Anthony Phillips the theological basis of punishment in the tribal era of Israelite history was the covenant between Yahweh and his chosen people. It was based on the treaty form of Hittite suzerainty. Yahweh filled the role of the king and the clans that of the vassal. Some of the clans had emerged from Egypt under the leadership of Moses, others had linked up in Canaan at a later date. They were united, not by a common ancestor, but by allegiance to the covenant God. The relationship between Yahweh and his covenant people is the predominant theme of these sacred writings, and penology is derived from it.[1]

The terms of the agreement were that Yahweh would afford divine protection and prosperity in return for their loyalty and devotion.

Any disloyalty or unfaithfulness would provoke his anger and bring swift reprisal. The mutual promises were written on tablets of stone and preserved in the 'ark of the covenant'. Periodically the agreement would be read before a large assembly. In the Sinai theophany Yahweh said to Moses:

> Now therefore if you will obey my voice and keep my covenant, you shall be my own possession among all peoples; for all the earth is mine (Ex. 19.5).

In order to prevent a breach of the covenant a number of stipulations were provided. The laws which enshrined Yahweh's requirement were said to have been laid down by divine revelation; but it is probable that they were largely a reflection of the moral standards of neighbouring communities, with certain insights which made them unique. It is usual to divide the laws into two categories: *apodictic* (with the prefix 'You shall not') and *casuistic* (with the prefix 'Suppose a man does'). The former were thought to be cultic and to have come from Yahweh, the latter to be secular and to have been borrowed from Canaanite law. The precise origin of both is uncertain. What is important is that they were believed to have come from Yahweh. They were written with the finger of God (Ex. 31.18). The obligations of the covenant were Israel's first code of criminal law.[2]

The Decalogue shows how closely the criminal law was associated with the obligations of the covenant.[3] The first five commandments are concerned with allegiance to Yahweh in a polytheistic environment: the remaining five refer to offences against the other members of the community. Any breach of the ten commandments amounted to an act of apostasy, and must be punished by the community in order to show its allegiance to Yahweh. Failure to repudiate the crime of the individual might provoke divine anger and threaten the security and prosperity of the amphictyony.

The first crime in the list is idolatry. 'You shall have no other gods before me' (Ex. 20.3). 'Whoever sacrifices to any god, save to the Lord only, shall be utterly destroyed' (Ex. 22.20). The second was the prohibition of images. 'You shall not make yourself a graven image or likeness of anything' (Ex. 20.4). In view of the fact that all the surrounding tribes used material objects, carved out of wood or moulded with metal, it was quite remarkable that Israel was expected to worship an imageless God. Some scholars believe this prohibition came into force long after the time of Moses.

The third commandment has to do with the improper use of the divine name. This is thought to refer, not so much to blasphemy, but to practices associated with magic, such as curses and spells. Later legislation rendered illegal every sort of occult practice. Yahweh was free to act as he pleased and must not be subject to manipulation by black magic. The fourth is an injunction to observe the sabbath day. How far back into history this statute goes is difficult to determine. There may have been sabbath observance in the wilderness period, but the reasons given for the rite are probably later additions.

The fifth is 'Honour your father and mother', and there is a further comment elsewhere which threatens 'Whoever strikes his father or his mother shall be put to death' and 'Whoever curses his father or his mother shall be put to death' (Ex. 20.12; 21.15, 17). Here there is a difference between the laws of Israel and those of Babylon. The latter said a son who assaulted his father should have a hand cut off. Israel's penalty was death. The protection of the family was an important aspect of the covenant relationship.

Of the crimes against their fellow-men the most serious was, of course, murder. For pre-meditated homicide the death penalty was automatic. There was no question of individual responsibility of the killer, there was no question of appeasing the family of the deceased, there was no question of buying off the supreme penalty or providing a substitute as a scape-goat. Blood belongs to God, and the shedding of blood is an insult to him. To propitiate him is the purpose of the extreme penalty. 'Whoever sheds the blood of man, by man shall his blood be shed' (Gen. 9.6).

Adultery is the next deviation to be condemned (Ex. 20.14). In some near-eastern countries this was a secular offence and the emphasis was on redress for the aggrieved husband, who was given wide discretion. For the Israelites it was a sacral matter. It was an offence to Yahweh and a repudiation of the covenant relationship. The death penalty was therefore mandatory. But do the laws reflect actual practice? Dr McKeating observes, 'It is worth noting that there is no recorded instance in the whole of Jewish narrative literature of the biblical period of anyone actually being put to death for adultery'.[4] Although the Deuteronomic code states 'If a man is found lying with the wife of another man, *both* of them shall die' (Deut. 22.22), it would seem that the husband was the injured party. The adulteress might be punished by being stripped naked in public

(Hos. 2.3) or even mutilated (Ezek. 23.25). Or the punishment could be left to God, as in the case of David and Bathsheba (II Sam. 12.13).

The commandment, 'You shall not steal' raises a problem. Theft of property was not a criminal offence in ancient Israel. It was a tort, dealt with in civil courts, where the culprit would be ordered to make restitution. What the eighth law is referring to, according to Anthony Phillips, is the offence of man-stealing. Selling an Israelite outside the covenant community, as was the case when the brothers of Joseph sold him to the Ishmaelite traders on their way to Egypt (Gen. 37.25–28), was equivalent to murder. Here is an interpretation of the Decalogue provision:

> If a man is found stealing one of his brethren, the people of Israel, and if he treats him as a slave or sells him, then that thief shall die; so you shall purge the evil from the midst of you (Deut. 24.7).

The ninth commandment prohibits false witness. 'You shall not bear false witness against your neighbour' (Ex. 20.16). The meaning here is not simple lying and deception, but giving untrue testimony in a murder trial and causing an innocent man to be executed. It was judicial murder and was punishable by death (Deut. 19.19). One way of avoiding such miscarriage of justice was to have two witnesses before a guilty verdict of a capital offence is reached. There is no evidence that witnesses had to take an oath to tell the truth, but this law shows a determination to protect the innocent from a miscarriage of justice.

The tenth commandment, which condemns covetousness, seems out of place in a code of criminal law, since it appears to refer to a mental attitude rather than an overt action. Dr Phillips tries to substantiate his theory by saying that the prohibition is concerned with depriving an elder of his status. The head of a household was an important person in the maintenance of law and order, and to dispossess him was regarded as a breach of the covenant and therefore a criminal offence.

Whether Phillips is right in saying that the Decalogue constituted Israel's criminal law in pre-exilic times is open to question, for exact chronological evidence is not provided in the literature. He admits that an ancient date for the code is not generally accepted and that some of the commandments are applicable to a later date. He also agrees that some of the laws, which he believes were given to Moses at

Sinai, were expanded in later years. His main contention is that this elementary code contained the stipulations of the covenant which brought the amphictyony into being, and that the death penalty was imposed for their breach.

Although the laws were attributed to divine revelation, their enforcement was the responsibility of the community. In the nomadic days there were no courts of justice, nor any police officers. The head of the family was responsible for the behaviour of his kindred, and there were clan leaders who formed a council for the settling of disputes. After the settlement in Canaan the elders met at the gate of the city to administer justice.

An illustration of how the head of a family sought to maintain discipline in his house is provided in the legend of Judah, the chief of one of the tribes. He married a Canaanite and had three sons. The eldest married Tamar, but because he was wicked Yahweh slew him and Tamar was left a widow. According to custom the second son, Onan, should have taken her to wife, but he refused to sire children for his dead brother. During the sheep-shearing season Judah had intercourse with a prostitute and agreed to present her with a goat, but she was not to be found. Three months later Tamar admitted that she had played the harlot and was pregnant by her father-in-law. Judah was ready to administer justice within the family. 'Bring her out,' he commanded, 'and let her be burned.' When he learnt that he was the father of his daughter-in-law's child, he said, 'She is more righteous than I.' Although he acknowledged his guilt, there is no record of his being punished (Gen. 38).

The punishments meted out to offenders against the laws were severe, showing how keenly the tribes felt about placating their deity. The most spectacular one was execution. Homicide was such a serious offence that nothing less than death could make good the breach of the covenant. The usual form of execution was stoning, which was carried out by the whole community, the accuser casting the first stone. The clan made a dramatic repudiation of the offence committed and divine reprisal was prevented.

The concept of blood-vengeance is one of the major features of punishment in ancient Israel. When a case of wilful murder occurred the kinsman of the victim had to avenge his death by killing the murderer. There had to be two witnesses and there was no question of accepting a payment in lieu of his life, for bloodshed defiled the land.

Expiation cannot be made on behalf of the land for blood shed on it except by the blood of the man that shed it (Num. 35.33).

The death penalty was inflicted for a number of other offences. As laid down in the Decalogue offences carrying the supreme sanction included sacrificing to other gods (Ex. 22.20), working on the sabbath day (Ex. 31.15), striking father or mother (Ex. 21.15) and stealing a man (Ex. 31.16). That stoning was a spectacular demonstration that the community repudiated the offence is illustrated in the story of Achan. After the fall of Jericho, Joshua laid down that there was to be no looting. Any spoil was to be devoted to Yahweh and 'utterly destroyed'. Achan defied the ban, took silver and gold and a mantle and hid them in the ground inside his tent. When the Israelite army was defeated in the next battle, they cast lots to find the guilty person. Achan was found out and convicted of offending Yahweh by his disobedience.

Swift execution followed. 'And all Israel stoned him with stones: they burned them with fire and stoned them with stones. And they raised over him a great heap of stones that remain to this day; then the Lord turned from his burning anger' (Josh. 7.16–26). The text is not very clear and opinions differ as to whether Achan's wife and children were put to death. If they were, there is added evidence that transgressing the covenant of the Lord was so shameful as to demand a vivid repudiation of the offence.

There is no case of execution by hanging in the annals of ancient Israel. There appears to·have been an instance of it in Egypt during the time of Joseph, but even that story is not without ambiguity. It is stated that his chief baker was hanged by Pharoah. It had been predicted by Joseph that 'Pharoah will lift up your head from you', and the phrase could equally refer to 'beheading', but it was also predicted that the baker's body 'would be hanged on a tree for the birds to eat the flesh' (Gen. 40.16–22).

Other cases of hanging the body on a tree recorded in the literature provide evidence that the repudiation of offences against the covenant were given spectacular demonstration. After the battle of Ai, Joshua hanged the body of the defeated king on a tree until evening (Josh. 8.29). When Joshua overcame the five kings of the Amorites he put them to death and hung them on five trees until the going down of the sun (Josh. 10.26–7). The practice of hanging bodies on trees continued into the period of the monarchy. Ishbosheth, son of Saul, was a threat to David's authority. When he was murdered in his bed by his two captains, David was angry, said he would require their blood for that of their victim, and had them killed; their hands and feet were cut off and they were hanged by the pool in Hebron (II Sam. 4.12).

It was usual to take down the bodies at sunset to prevent the vultures from devouring the flesh, though in the case of Saul's sons and grandsons the bodies were left hanging until the drought ended. They were protected from the birds of prey and the beasts by Rizpah, Saul's concubine (II Sam. 21.10). It was because the drought was a sign of Yahweh's displeasure at the slaughter of the Gibeonites that there was need for a striking display of penitential grief. The words, 'Cursed be every one that hangs upon a tree' had a special significance for Paul (Gal. 3.13). The criminal who was hanged on a tree was indeed cursed.

Scholars who explore the origins of punishment in the experience of primitive tribes have elicited some features which they think explain how penal systems began. The first is that the infliction of pain on the offender was a device for cooling down the outrage felt by the victim of a criminal act. When a person is injured, deprived or humiliated he feels bitter and resentful, and the best way to pacify him was to punish the offender. In his book on the history of penal methods, George Ives expresses this view succinctly:

> The placation of the injured party was the objective of the oldest laws[5].

Henry Maine supports this view:

> It is curious to observe how little men of primitive times were troubled with scruples (as to the degree of moral guilt to be ascribed to the wrong-doer) and how completely they were persuaded that the impulses of the wronged person were the proper measure of vengeance he was entitled to exact, and how literally they imitated the rise and fall of his passions in fixing the scale of punishment.[6]

Another factor which is said to be the earliest impulse in the aetiology is the instinct of retaliation. This was expressed by Robert R. Marett, 'The earliest function of law was to control retaliation.'[7] According to this theory private vengeance was taken over by the community in order that it might be limited to reasonable proportions. Punishment is explained as an expression of an instinctive urge to hit back when injured. If the victim of an attack should be unable to avenge himself his next of kin was expected to do it for him. Private reprisals were often out of all proportion to the damage done by the original offence, so revenge was taken over by the legal authorities. Instead of a penalty fixed by the caprice of the injured party, there was legal provision to limit vengeance to what the rulers thought was reasonable.

In view of this widely accepted theory it is necessary to consider the *lex talionis*, which is often thought to be the most fundamental principle of the Mosaic legislation. The relevant passages are often quoted as if they were a complete statement of Old Testament teaching on punishment. They are believed to show that the limitation of revenge was the salient feature of Israel's penal code. These are some of the pericopes which express this principle:

> You shall give life for life, eye for eye, tooth for tooth, hand for hand, foot for foot, burn for burn, wound for wound, stripe for stripe (Ex. 21.23–5).

> Your eye shall not pity; it shall be life for life, eye for eye, tooth for tooth, hand for hand, foot for foot (Deut. 19.21).

> When a man causes a disfigurement in his neighbour, as he has done it shall be done to him, fracture for fracture, eye for eye, tooth for tooth; as he has disfigured a man so shall he be disfigured (Lev. 24.19–20).

The similarity between Israelite legislation and the code of Hammurabi, king of Babylon, which dates from about 1,700 BC is striking. The Babylonian judgments were said to be given by the sun-god Shamash and they embrace 248 laws. A few extracts will illustrate the point:

> If a man has caused the loss of a gentleman's eye, his own eye shall one cause to be lost.

> If a man has made the tooth of a man that is his equal to fall out, one shall make his tooth fall out.

> If a builder has built a house for a man and has not made strong his work, and the house has fallen and he has caused the death of the owner of the house, that builder shall be put to death.

> If it is the son or slave that has been killed, then the son or slave of the builder shall be put to death.[8]

Revenge limited and controlled by law was clearly a phenomenon well known in the world at the time when Moses claimed to have received the law from Yahweh on Mount Sinai, but it is by no means certain that it affected that law. The Mosaic doctrine of blood-vengeance was very different from simple retaliation. In fact Dr Phillips has expressed the view that the *lex talionis* passages are post-exilic interpolations, implying that retaliation was not a major principle of Israel's criminal law in the early centuries.

The religious character of punishment in Israel has been emphasized by Leslie Davison:

> From earliest times punishment was a corporate action carried out by authorized persons for the protection of the tribe. Any breach of custom disrupted the harmony and threatened the survival of the group. The transgression of the individual exposed the whole population to the immeasurable anger of supernatural agencies.[9]

Whilst there may have been an element of proportionate retaliation in some of the penalties of the Israelite code, the most glaring anomalies for the modern reader are the extremely severe sanctions for crimes which seem trivial by today's moral standards. In the case of the sabbath-breaker, for instance, the punishment is out of all proportion to the guilt incurred. The text runs as follows:

> When the people of Israel were in the wilderness, they found a man gathering sticks on the sabbath day. And those who found him gathering sticks brought him to Moses and Aaron, and to all the congregation. They put him in custody, because it had not been made plain what should be done to him. And the Lord said to Moses 'The man shall be put to death: all the congregation shall stone him with stones outside the camp.' And all the congregation brought him outside the camp, and stoned him to death with stones, as the Lord had commanded Moses (Num. 15.32–36).

The law was quite explicit, 'Whoever does any work on the sabbath day shall be put to death' (Ex. 31.15). The *lex talionis* was not operating in a case like this. The same could be said regarding capital punishment for striking a parent. Whereas the Babylonian code said that a son who assaults his father shall have a hand cut off, Israelite law prescribed execution. Respect for the head of the family was an obligation to Yahweh (Ex. 21.15).

One of the implications of this theological basis for punishment would seem to be that the individual offender could be sacrificed for the supposed safety of the whole community, so it is not surprising that many deplore what seems to be a violation of human rights. It was in an attempt to resolve this anomaly that Wheeler Robinson posited a development in Israelite thinking from what he called the notion of 'corporate personality' to a belief in individual responsibility. The killing of Achan's family for Achan's sin is the best known illustration of the theory that the individual's well-being could be ignored as long as the tribe was preserved. Other examples are the killing of Saul's descendants as a reprisal for the king's slaughter of the Gibeonites. In the modern eye it seems immoral to punish the innocent for the crimes of the guilty.

This problem has been discussed at some length by Paul Joyce[10] who repudiates Robinson's claim that the individual Israelite was not held responsible for his own deeds until the sixth century BC when the exilic prophet Ezekiel offered a categorical and dogmatic statement that each individual is responsible for his own deeds. It is clear, Joyce says, that there was individual responsibility under Israel's criminal law in early times, and it is equally clear that today we personify communities, like nations, clubs or other groups, as if they were units.

Joyce says we have to distinguish between language about criminal law on the human level and language about divine punishment of human sin. Under the Israelite penal system only the guilty person is punished. The individual offender is regarded as responsible for his own actions, as is seen in the provision that only the death of the murderer himself can expiate the crime. There was no demand for vicarious punishment. The idea was put forward by Ruskin that in the case of a murderer an inhabitant of the area should be chosen by lot and hanged so as to encourage the whole community to keep the peace.[11] Such a suggestion would have been inconceivable in Israel. There certainly was recognition of individual accountability in the criminal law of Israel.[12]

With divine punishment of human sin, however, the situation is different. The anger of Yahweh could be directed towards the whole community, or towards individuals within it. There could be defeat in battle, as in the case of Joshua's defeat at Ai, or famine, as in the reign of David. Because this king had sinned against the Lord his child died (II Sam. 12.14–23). There is frequent repetition of the formula, 'visiting the iniquity of the fathers upon the children to the third and fourth generation of those who hate me' (Ex. 20.5; 34.7; Num. 14.18; Deut. 5.9 etc.). This indicates the absolute nature of God's judgment, which could entail the annihilation of a whole family. Yahweh was free to punish indiscriminately the whole tribe or nation.

On one occasion the Lord sent a pestilence upon Israel and the death toll was seventy thousand men, and David acknowledged his own guilt but added, 'These sheep, what have they done? Let thy hand be against me and my father's house' (II Sam. 24.15–17). The sin of Manasseh was said to have caused the fall of Jerusalem (II Kings 23.26–27). Abraham had to plead with Yahweh not to slay the righteous with the wicked in Sodom (Gen. 18.25). Jeremiah declares that because of the sins of the people, 'the young men shall die by the sword; their sons and their daughters shall die by famine' (Jer. 11.22). Women would be widowed and childless as a judgment of God (Jer. 18.21).

Natural disasters are still called acts of God, and in earlier times the adverse elements were seen as weapons in the hand of the tribal deity. Thunder, lightning, earthquake and volcanic eruption caused the people to tremble with fear (Ex. 20.18). Shortage of water was a constant threat to their very existence. Drought and disease were formidable sanctions against families struggling to survive. Ignorance of natural law and absence of agricultural technology invited superstitious ideas, so it is not surprising that natural events were seen as visitations of the deity. When, for example, Korah organized an insurrection against Moses and Aaron 'the ground under them split asunder and the earth opened its mouth and swallowed them up, with all their households, and all that belonged to the rebels went down into Sheol; the earth closed over them and they perished from the midst of the assembly' (Num. 16.29–35).

Given this theological climate it is hardly surprising that any act which provoked divine anger called for swift and ruthless punishment. The aim of the penal provisions was to propitiate Yahweh and prevent the calamity which would follow a breach of the covenant relationship and threaten the very existence of the amphictyony. The religious significance of punishment is one of the major facts to emerge from the study of vengeance in the penal history of Israel.

The defenders of the progressive revelation theory could take refuge in the view that there was a theological transformation in later periods to a less capricious concept of the character of God which affected penal practice. There were some, on the other hand, who still saw illness as a punishment for the sins of ancestors. Even the disciples of Jesus asked concerning a man blind from his birth, 'Rabbi, who sinned, this man or his parents, that he was born blind?' (John 9.2). There were many views regarding the justification of punishment in the Old Testament, just as there are today.

Some scholars argue that we are living in a sinful world and that capital punishment, though not the original will of God, is a sign of divine accommodation to the sinfulness of man. They say the law is an interim arrangement for the present aeon. Thielicke argues that the survival of the chosen race was necessary to salvation history. Drastic measures were needed in primitive times to maintain the covenant. That God preserved the tribes, whatever the cost, was a sign of his mercy. It was a miracle of his grace that he refused to let man destroy himself. He quotes the incident in which Francis Drake commanded his mutinous lieutenant to be executed for the sake of discipline and the survival of the crew, but partook of the holy communion with him in the greatest fraternity before giving the order for his death.[13]

Other experts reach the conclusion that there is no difference in the revelation as between the Old Testament and the New. According to A. A. Van Ruler, 'The New Testament brings no new and independent revelatory event as compared with the Old Testament'.[14] The pre-existent Christ is seen as lord of the Old Testament as well as the New. The divine mercy which operated in the experience of ancient Israel is identical to that proclaimed by the apostles.

The other view is that the true character of God was only partially understood by primitive peoples. The revelation in Jesus Christ is of a God of love and some theologians see no possibility of reconciling the radical ethic of the gospel with the crude penalties of the early Israelite code. This dilemma is one of the main problems to be faced by the student of punishment in the Bible.

2 THE CONCEPT OF JUSTICE

Another theological idea which prompted the theory and practice of punishment in the history of Israel is that of justice. It is not necessary to determine how it fits into a chronological scheme or whether it was part of a development process. It might be the case that it was held by some people throughout the whole period, for the dating of the literature is a precarious process. On the other hand it appears to have been uppermost during the era of the monarchy.[1]

The idea is that God had created the world in such a way that communities could only prosper and survive if they observed certain moral principles. Built into the natural order of the universe was the principle that goodness would bring prosperity and wickedness would bring adversity. This was grounded in the character of God himself, who was a moral being, and it was his will that good would triumph over evil. In a moral universe things would work God's way or there would be dire consequences. The goodness of the Creator was manifest in his fair treatment of man.

In the name of their God, who demanded obedience to his laws, the prophets of the eighth century BC thundered their denunciations of wickedness. Amos was sure that drought and pestilence were divine punishments, showing God's disapproval of their life style. There are inevitable consequences of wrong-doing. 'Does a lion roar in the forest when he has no prey?' (Amos 3.4; 4.7–10). Likewise the Deuteronomists had a clear-cut theory of God's dealings with men. People were either good or bad, and punishments were meted out to the bad and rewards to the good. A major quality in the make-up of the deity was justice (Deut. 13.12–18).

When God threatened to destroy Sodom and Gomorrah with fire and brimstone, Abraham asked the question, 'Shall not the judge of all the earth do right?' He then challenged divine justice by saying that the righteous should not be slain with the wicked (Gen. 18.25). Here was an attempt to probe the righteousness of God. Justice demanded that God should not punish the innocent. Punishment was only just when it was related to guilt.

It was upon this pattern of divine justice in God's treatment of his people that a system of criminal justice for the community was to be established. If it were God's will that people should be treated fairly there must be protection of people's rights and punishment should be related to guilt. In a theocratic society those appointed to rule are God's agents and are expected to imitate him in their ordering of society.

When the Israelite tribes entered Canaan and settled down to agricultural and city life, the need for a more sophisticated system of justice became apparent. Complaints were made that 'every one did what was right in his own eyes' (Judg. 21.25). The story of the rape of the Levite's concubine illustrates this unsatisfactory situation. This man and his partner were guests in the home of a farmer, when some base fellows arrived and demanded that the visitor come out in order that they might *know* him. The farmer offered them his own virgin daughter and the visitor's concubine and begged them to leave the Levite alone. When they refused, he pushed the concubine out to them and locked the door. They abused her all night and when dawn broke she was found on the door-step – unconscious.

The Levite put her upon his ass and went home. Then he took a knife, divided her limb from limb into twelve parts and sent them throughout all the territory of Israel. All who saw it said: 'Such a thing has never happened or been seen from the day that the people of Israel came up out of the land of Egypt until this day; consider it, take counsel and speak' (Judg. 19). What they were expected to say when they did speak was that the base fellows who had abused the girl should have been given an appropriate punishment. It was surely not right in the eyes of God that a person was sacrificed to satisfy the lusts of scoundrels of the tribe of Benjamin.[2]

One school of thought in Israel believed that the institution of the monarchy would provide a system of justice which would be acceptable to God. Samuel had done his best but when his sons were appointed judges in Beersheba they took bribes and perverted justice. The discipline of family courts and the adjudications of the elders at the city gate had proved inadequate. There was need for a national system of justice, which would guarantee the punishment of the wicked and the well-being of the good. The enthronement of a king would achieve this end (I Sam. 8.3–19).

It was with some reluctance that Samuel found them a king. Saul, of the tribe of Benjamin was tall and handsome and came of a wealthy family, and he was invited to a banquet where he was anointed with oil and told that God had chosen him to reign over his people. At a solemn assembly of the tribes Saul was proclaimed king, but there was a minority group who despised him, saying, 'How can this man save us?' (I Sam. 10).

It was with some difficulty that Saul established his authority. After a battle against the Philistines he ordered a fast to be observed by all the people. His own son, Jonathan, defied the command and ate some honey, whereupon the new king ordered his execution, but the people refused to endorse this verdict. 'Not one hair of his head shall fall to the ground,' they said. 'So the people ransomed Jonathan and he did not die' (II Sam. 8.15).

The king's authority was sorely tried again when Ahimelech and the priests at Nob gave a sword and food to David, who was an outlaw and was gaining popularity in opposition to Saul. The royal order was that the priests be slain, but his servants refused to put forth their hands to kill the priests of the Lord. The attempt at kingly rule was frustrated. However, Doeg the Edomite was ready to carry out the execution, and he slaughtered eighty-five priests and proceeded to put to the sword all the inhabitants of the city of Nob, men, women, children, sucklings, oxen, asses and sheep (I Sam. 22.11–19).

The king was seen as God's representative on earth, was expected to enforce laws which had been given by divine command, had to commend himself to the populace and to work harmoniously with the religious leaders. In addition his fitness to rule was gauged by his ability to administer justice and equity throughout the land. Eventually Saul broke down under the strain, became mentally ill, and was told by Samuel that he had been rejected by God.

His successor, David, was not heir to the throne by heredity, but was selected by Samuel and approved by the people. One of his chief qualifications for the position was that he would establish law and order in his realm. Indeed, the chronicler at a later date stated categorically, 'So David reigned over all Israel and administered justice and equity to all the people' (I Chron. 18.14).

The ideal view of the king as judge was well known in the Near East at that time.[3] It was generally agreed that justice was part of the natural order of things and that a king's primary duty was to guarantee that it would be impartially executed in the community. To create right social relationships and care for the underprivileged was an acknowledged royal responsibility. As Isaiah put it, a true king is one who 'judges and seeks justice and is swift to do righteousness (16.5).

Before David was actually crowned[4] he had to show what was meant by justice and equity. Three brothers were involved in a case of blood vengeance. The saga began when one of them, Asahel, who was as swift of foot as a wild gazelle, was brutally murdered by Abner the commander of Saul's army. He smote him in the belly with his spear, so that the spear came out at his back, and he died (II Sam. 2.23).

When Abner returned to Hebron, Joab, brother of the murdered Asahel, decided he must avenge his brother's death. He took Abner aside to speak to him privately and smote him in the belly, and he died for the blood of his brother (II Sam. 3.26–30). This killing of Abner was illegal, because his slaying of Asahel was carried out in time of war. David took no action against Joab, though he deplored what he had done. He attended Abner's funeral, wept at the grave and tasted no bread that day until the sun went down. He said, 'The Lord requite the evil-doer according to his wickedness' (II Sam. 3.39).[5]

David's successor had no scruples about the matter, and he quickly ordered the execution of Joab for the blood he had shed. The chief of the army went immediately and killed him, and buried him in his house in the wilderness (I Kings 2.28–35). There was another reason for Joab's death. He had supported Adonijah in his struggle to succeed David on the throne. Political intrigue was closely bound up with the ostensible administration of justice. The authority to rule and maintain order in the nation was obtained by assassinations. Justice may have been an ideal, but it was not often realized during the monarchy in Israel.

Another example of the mixture of politics and justice came at the time of Saul's death. News that the throne was now vacant was brought to David at Ziklag by an Amalekite messenger. He reported that Saul, badly wounded in battle, had implored him to take his life. Thinking he was doing David a favour, the Amalekite had brought the royal crown and the arm-band. To his surprise David sentenced him to death on the charge that, by his own admission, he had slain the Lord's anointed. The Amalekite was killed on the spot (II Sam. 1.1–16). Earlier it was stated that Saul had taken his own life by falling upon his sword (I Sam. 31.4).[6]

One very significant element in the monarchic system was that appeal could be made from the local court to a higher authority. Presumably the elders at the gate continued to function and there were judges sitting in various courts throughout the land, though there is little evidence regarding the cases they dealt with. The new court of appeal may have restricted the power of the city magistrates and was clearly a significant addition to the judicial machinery.

Examples of how the appeal system worked are given in two fictitious cases in which the judgment of the king was sought during David's reign. The first is the parable which Nathan the prophet put to David for his comments. A rich man had many flocks and herds, while a poor man had only one little ewe lamb. When the rich man had a visitor for dinner, he stole the poor man's pet lamb instead of killing one of his own. What did the king in his judicial capacity think of that?

David was very angry. 'As the Lord lives,' he thundered, 'the man who has done this deserves to die; and he shall restore the lamb fourfold, because he did this thing and because he had no pity' (II Sam. 12.5–6). The king's outburst might be taken to imply that the lower court, which could treat the act of sheep-stealing only as a tort and not as a crime, was inadequate to deal with so glaring an injustice. Although the man deserved to die the law was to be upheld and the verdict was 'four-fold restitution'.

Nathan then accused David of the murder of Uriah the Hittite and of adultery with Uriah's wife. Although he had committed two capital offences – murder and adultery – the ruler was above the law. He showed great penitence. 'I have sinned against the Lord,' he confessed: but the law applied only to his subjects and not to the monarch himself (II Sam.12.12). On the other hand the prophet said he could not escape *divine* punishment. The sword would never depart from his house, his wives would be ravaged and the son of his adulterous intercourse would die.[7]

The second example is a case which was brought by the Tekoite widow. One of her sons had killed his brother in a quarrel and the family was demanding blood vengeance. They had ordered her to give up the murderer so that he could be slain for his brother's life. If she agreed the family would be wiped out; but if the king would grant a pardon the dead man's blood would be upon her and not upon the king.

David was inclined to defer judgment, for she admitted that there had been no witnesses to the murder, but when she persisted the king swore that not one hair of her son's head would fall to the ground. The elders at the gate would not have power to commute the death sentence, but the king could overthrow the verdict of the local magistrates. The widow then revealed that the case was fictitious. She explained that the king's own son, Absalom, was guilty of the premeditated murder of Amnon and was in exile in order to avoid blood vengeance. Why should he not be pardoned? The king ordered that Absalom be brought back to Jerusalem, but he must live in a separate house and not in the palace. For two years David never saw his son.

Meanwhile Absalom began a campaign to seize the throne from his father and the method he adopted was significant for the doctrine of the 'just king'. He would rise early in the morning and stand by the city gate, and when an aggrieved party had a suit to bring before the king he would deal with it himself. He would give every man justice. To administer justice and equity to all the people was the justification for kingly rule. The king was the protector of the underprivileged. That Absalom competed with David in hearing complaints seems to show that the nation's supreme judge was not fulfilling his role adequately (II Sam. 14).

David's successor was Solomon and he was regarded as the 'just king' *par excellence*. Soon after he came to the throne he had a dream in which God granted him a wish. He said he wanted an understanding mind to govern the people on moral principles. He wanted to perceive when an accused person was guilty or innocent. So God granted his wish. An opportunity to exercise his powers of perception soon came. Two harlots came to him for a judgment. One of them had given birth to a child, and three days later the other was delivered of her baby. One child died and his mother stole the other child and swore it was her own. How would the king decide which woman was telling a lie?

Solomon was equal to the task. He took a sword and ordered the living child to be cut in half, so that the two harlots might share the disputed offspring. The deceitful woman agreed, but the honest woman wanted the child spared even if it was taken from her. The king then gave the baby to its rightful mother. 'And all Israel heard of the judgment and stood in awe of the king because they perceived that the wisdom of God was with him to render justice' (I Kings 3.28).

The concept of the 'just king' was severely shaken after the kingdom was divided and Ahab was ruler of the Northern Kingdom with his capital at Samaria. Naboth owned a vineyard close to the palace and the king wanted to buy it, but the owner refused. Queen Jezebel determined to facilitate the acquisition of the property. She arranged for false witnesses to accuse Naboth of cursing God and the king. This was treason, for there was a law which said, 'You shall not revile God nor curse a ruler of your people'. Naboth was taken outside the city and stoned to death (I Kings 21).

Ahab's abuse of his political authority was denounced by the prophet Elijah. Retribution would follow and in the very place where dogs licked the blood of Naboth, they would eventually lick the king's blood, he said. A later record says the two sons of Naboth were stoned along with their father, but this may have been an attempt to show how Ahab was able to appropriate the property, which was not transferable as long as there were descendants to inherit it (II Kings 9.26).

Ordinary people were able to approach the king if they were the victims of injustice. During the siege of Samaria, when famine conditions prevailed in the city, the king appeared on the wall and was approached by a woman who was crying for help. Driven by intense hunger two women had agreed to eat their own children on successive days, but her partner had gone back on her word and hidden her son. There appears to have been no legal provision for such a contingency and there was nothing the king could do about it (II Kings 6.24–27).

On another occasion the king was approached by a widow who had gone into Philistine territory to escape the famine; and when she returned she wanted to reclaim her house and land. The king appointed an official to see that the Shunamite woman, whose son Elisha had raised from the dead, recovered all her property (II Kings 8.1–6).

The king had the power of life and death in Israel. There is a juridical parable. King Ahab was approached by a prophet, who was wearing a bandage over his eyes. He said he had been given a prisoner of war to guard and had allowed him to escape. What was the king's judgment? Ahab said the prophet must be put to death or pay a talent of silver. The prophet removed the bandage and accused the king of allowing Benhadad, king of Syria, to escape after he had been captured in battle (I Kings 20.39–43).

Some of the criticisms of the monarchs may well have been lodged by historians who were opposed to the monarchy on principle. Dr Rogerson has called attention to Assyrian records in which Omri, one of the kings of Israel, who fortified the hill of Samaria, is highly praised for keeping his country strong and stable, yet the Deuteronomist writer dismisses him in seven verses, saying that he did more evil in the sight of the Lord than all who were before him (I Kings 16.21–28).[8] There was evidence, however, that some of the monarchs had been arbitrary in their judgments, frequently ruthless, regarding themselves as above the law, and did outrageous things. Some of them had provoked the condemnation of the prophets and it is not surprising that one school of thought expressed the view that the monarchy had been a mistake from the start (I Sam. 8).

There was something to be said on the credit side. When you try to assess the ethical significance of social policies in the ancient world, the criteria have to be related in some measure to current standards. Archaeology has provided evidence which enables the historian to compare Israel's penal system with those of the surrounding nations. We have seen that the covenant relationship with Yahweh legitimized severe penalties for certain sacral offences, such as gathering firewood on the sabbath day (Num. 15.32). Israelite law was also severe on a son striking a parent, the penalty being death, whereas the law of ancient Babylon prescribed the cutting off of the hand for that offence (Ex. 21.15).[9]

The penal system under the monarchy compared well with the practice of Israel's neighbours. How far the kings were responsible for humanitarian developments is not easy to determine. Certainly there were features of Israel's law which were commendable even by modern standards of justice. One of these was the provision for dealing with offences against property. Whereas the code of Hammurabi in Babylon imposed the death penalty for stealing, there is no evidence that taking another person's goods was a capital offence in Israel.

One significant principle of justice in the Old Testament is that people matter more than property. In no case does the protection of material goods *per se* concern Israel's *criminal* law. Stealing was a tort – a breach of duty liable to entail a claim for damages. The civil court would settle disputes by ordering restitution. For example:

When fire breaks out and catches the thorns so that the stacked grain or the standing grain or the field is consumed, he that kindled the fire shall make full restitution (Ex. 22.6).

Now simple restitution according to the damage done would have no deterrent value, so the payment demanded might be two-fold or even as much as seven-fold of the cost of restoration. Thus:

> If a man steals an ox or a sheep, and kills it or sells it, he shall pay five oxen for an ox, and four sheep for a sheep. . . . If the stolen beast is found alive in his possession, whether it is an ox or an ass or a sheep, he shall pay double (Ex. 22.1–4).

The law provided for corporal punishment to be inflicted under certain circumstances. It was assumed that a father would chastise a rebellious son (Deut. 21.18–21) and the elders of the city could order whipping for the man who falsely accused his bride of not being a virgin (Deut. 22.13–18). The most interesting case of beating is that where the man, found guilty of an offence and deserving punishment, shall be ordered to *lie down* and be beaten in the presence of the judge with a number of stripes in proportion to his offence. The number could be up to a maximum of forty, not more 'lest . . . your brother be degraded in your sight' (Deut. 25.1–3). Later the number was fixed at thirty-nine to prevent the maximum being exceeded (II Cor. 11.24). That the strokes of the cane were administered while the culprit was lying down would seem to be evidence that they were addressed to the soles of the feet, a common type of punishment among the Hebrews and the Egyptians.[10]

Bodily mutilation was also common among ancient peoples. It was not unknown for criminals to have their hands or feet cut off, and for more serious crimes they might have their eyes put out, or their nose, ears or lips might be cut off.[11] One case is mentioned in Israel's law and it is unlikely that it was ever enforced:

> When men fight with one another, and the wife of one draws near to rescue her husband from the hand of him who is beating him, and puts out her hand and seizes him by the private parts, then you shall *cut off her hand*: your eye shall have no pity (Deut. 25.11–12).

There had always been a keen sense of individual responsibility for criminal acts in Israel's judicial system, but it was the Deuteronomists who made it clear that women were culpable in the eyes of the law and especially when sex offences with men were at issue. It seemed to be a humanizing of justice, but it is strange that bodily mutilation applied only to a woman. To ascribe individual responsibility to women may have been an aspect of feminine liberation, but it also meant that in a case of adultery the woman as well as the man must be put to death (Deut. 22.22; Lev. 20.10).

Israelite law showed a semblance of justice in its protection of slaves. How far back slavery goes in ancient times is not clear, but it would seem that part of the machinery of justice was that a man could be sold as a slave if he was in debt. A thief may have been ordered to make restitution and be unable to find the money or he may have borrowed money and his creditor is demanding repayment; then he could be offered for sale (Ex. 22.1–3). Elisha is said to have performed a miracle in order to help a woman whose two children were about to be taken as slaves by a money-lender (II Kings 4.1–7).

But even slaves had their rights and their dignity. Man was made in the image of God (Gen. 1.26) and that principle meant that even when a poor man was actually owned by a rich man there were human values which could not be cast aside. So laws were provided for the protection of slaves. They were not to be brutally treated by their masters; they were to be assured of the necessities of life; they were to be allowed to join the family for meals and worship and they must be permitted to rest on the sabbath day.

Slaves must not be ill-treated:

> When a man strikes his slave, male or female, with a rod and the slave dies under his hand, he shall be punished (Ex. 21.20).

> When a man strikes the eye of a slave, male or female, and destroys it, he shall let the slave go free for the eye's sake. If he knocks out the tooth of his slave, male or female, he shall let the slave go free for the tooth's sake (Ex. 21.26–27).

Israelites were not forced to remain in slavery on a permanent basis. After six years they must be liberated. Even during the six years of his captivity a slave could be redeemed by one of his brothers or by some near relative; or he could redeem himself, the price being adjusted according to how long he had been in bondage. He could also receive wages at half the rate paid to a hired servant (Deut. 15.18). If he had been treated well the slave might not wish to be set free, in which case he would have his ear pierced with an awl against the door for identification (Deut. 15.16–17). A slave could even inherit his master's property or share it as if he were one of the family (Gen. 15.3. Prov. 17.2).

On the matter of releasing a slave there is a difference of opinion as to whether a slave can take his wife and family with him when he is set free. One book states that if his master has provided him with a wife since he came in as a slave he must leave her and the children behind when he goes out to freedom (Ex. 21.1–6). This scarcely smacks of justice or human rights. The other account is silent on such a contingency. Does this mean that the forcible separation of a man from his wife and children was repudiated in a later code of law (Deut. 15.16–17)?

A more sanguine note still is struck in the cause of justice by the reform which seems to have been carried out during the reign of king Josiah; namely, that a released slave must not go out empty-handed. Previously there had been no provision for the material needs of liberated slaves. It had become clear that if they went from their master in poverty they would probably soon be back again. They were simply exchanging security without freedom for freedom without security. The new legislation instructed the master to furnish them liberally from his flock, his threshing floor and his winepress (Deut. 15.13–14).

There is something commendable about the directions for dealing with a runaway slave:

> You shall not give him up to his master . . . he shall dwell with you in your midst, in the place where he shall choose, within one of your towns, where it pleases him best; you shall not oppress him (Deut. 23.15–16).

To shelter and support a runaway slave was a sure sign that the whole system of slavery was being called into question; 'Hide the outcasts, betray not the fugitive,' was Isaiah's injunction (16.3). Another sign was the threat of the death penalty for abducting an Israelite in order to sell him into bondage (Ex. 21.16; Deut. 24.7). Loss of freedom was a legitimate punishment but a slave remained a human being with inalienable rights. The people were frequently reminded that their ancestors were once slaves in Egypt.

Prisoners of war also had their rights. A prophet named Oded rebuked the army of Israel on one occasion for threatening to subjugate as slaves thousands of women and children of men slain in battle. The unfortunate company were fed and clothed and sent back to their homes in Jericho (II Chron. 28.8–15). Historians say that the practice of condemning certain criminals to forced labour was universal in the middle-east[12] but this did not obtain among the Israelites.

There were cases in which aliens were conscripted to perform community service. Soon after the entry of the tribes into Canaan the Gibeonites used deception in order to obtain a treaty and Joshua cursed them and said 'Some of you shall always be slaves, hewers of wood and drawers of water for the house of God (Josh. 9.22–23). When David defeated the Ammonites at Rabbah he took the inhabitants and set them to labour with saws and iron picks and axes and made them toil at the brick kilns (II Sam. 12.31 cf. I Chron. 20.3). Solomon made a levy of forced labour to build the temple in Jerusalem, but these men were aliens (I Kings 9.15–22).

Another attempt to humanize justice in Israel was the provision of cities of refuge. Whereas in the nomadic era fugitives from justice had become outlaws in the desert, a new system for their protection in the urban situation came into being.

> When you cross the Jordan into the land of Canaan, then you shall select cities to be cities of refuge for you, that the manslayer who kills any person without intent may flee there (Num. 35.10–11).

An example of what might happen is given: a man is cutting down trees in the forest. The axe-head slips from the handle and kills his neighbour. The avenger of blood, in hot anger, will pursue him, overtake him and wound him mortally, though he did not deserve to die. The unintentional killer will make for the city of refuge and be given protection until a judicial trial can be arranged. There were six such cities spread over the land so as to prevent innocent blood being shed (Deut. 19.1–10).

If blood vengeance was a barbarous procedure, at least it could be said that an attempt was being made to bring it under the control of a system of justice. Normally a fugitive could not be dragged from the altar where he had sought sanctuary. He must be protected until a judicial hearing of the case could be arranged. It is true that Adonijah was dragged from the altar, but he was trying to usurp the throne and was later killed by Benaiah (I Kings 1.49–53). The cities of refuge represent an attempt to inflict punishment only when guilt had been established in a court of law. Punishment was still severe, and the purpose was that the public would *hear and fear* (Deut. 17.13; 19.20; 21.21).

In spite of the endeavours of successive monarchs to devise a system of justice, so that the sense of outrage felt by victims of crime could be brought under political control, there was much dissatisfaction with the results. The prophets were critical because human justice bore no relation to the justice of God upon which it was supposed to be based. Amos denounced those who dethroned justice, took bribes and thrust aside the poor when they came to the courts for redress (5.12). Isaiah accused the political leaders of being more interested in getting rich than in seeking the moral welfare of the nation (1.23).

Micah declared that what God required was that the people 'do justice, love kindness and walk humbly with God' (6.8). He alleged that the rulers abhorred justice and took bribes in giving judgments (3.9–11). The psalmist refers to men whose 'right hands are full of bribes' (26.10). The victims of criminal acts could have little confidence in the administration of justice if judgments could be bought by the rich at the expense of the poor. The existence of inequality in society made it impossible for perfect justice to be dispensed in the nation. The monarchy was discredited, but the prophets went on hoping for an ideal king who would be a true regent and worthy representative of God the righteous ruler of the Israelite state (Isa. 11.1–5).

The anti-monarchists looked back to the theocratic emphasis which had characterized earlier times. But it was not only that urbanization had brought social problems, it was equally the effect which the concept of the mighty king had on the Israelite doctrine of God. The potentate theology was to provide a theodicy which has influenced western religions ever since.[13] Sin was seen as rebellion against the rule of the mighty God who had the power of life and death and would punish disaffection with great ferocity. The doctrine of the all-powerful judge operating retribution co-incided with that of the just king. They doubtless appeared concurrently – the one having a bearing on the other.

Jeremiah proclaimed the nation would be punished by a righteous God and he agonized over the suffering which the Babylonian invasion of his country entailed. Resistance was futile. It was the inevitable result of sin. He was regarded as a traitor and was under house arrest. He had hoped that a just king would provide justice in the land. He now ponders over the question: 'Why does the way of the wicked prosper? (12.1). The suffering of the innnocent seemed to contradict all that the monarchy had stood for.

3 PUNISHMENT AND RECONCILIATION

The third theological concept which had a bearing on Old Testament penology is that of reconciliation. There is a sense in which this motive is present in the vengeance and justice models also, since to propitiate the deity and to give the guilty their due are as a secondary effect designed to create social harmony. When reconciliation to God and one's fellow men, however, is the paramount objective, punishment takes on a different character and may even be abrogated altogether.

Although this notion may not be identified with any period of Israelite history, there were certain writers with deep insight and powerful humanitarian impulses who saw that punishment could be used for the improvement of character and that mercy was a potent weapon for transforming behaviour. To imagine that the cutting to pieces of Agag and the dashing of children against the rocks is typical of Old Testament penology is a grievous error. Shining through the variety of theological viewpoints is the basic theme that God's mercy guiding, protecting and redeeming his people, is a secure foundation for the people's gracious treatment of one another.[1]

An early glimpse of divine mercy occurs in the story of Cain, who is reported to be the world's first murderer. Cain killed his brother Abel, whose blood cried out from the ground for vengeance. Surely the murderer should be stoned to death. Should we not expect that blood vengeance or retribution would demand the death penalty for a murderer? There was even a comment about the possibility of seven-fold vengeance (Gen. 4.24), but Cain was not executed, he was banished. He would be a fugitive and a wanderer on the earth and he would be branded so that no one would take his life (Gen. 4).

Whether this narrative belongs to history or myth, the thread in the vicious circle of revenge is broken by an act of mercy.[2]

Speculation about Cain's descendants may carry the lesson a little further. It has been suggested that Cain was the father of the Kenites, a wandering tribe of tinkers who were treated as outcasts and despised; but they also were protected and their persons treated as sacrosanct. It is even suggested that Yahweh was their tribal God and that Moses not only married a member of their community but shaped his theology on the basis of their faith. If the conjecture is true the concern for outcasts is understandable.[3]

Another glimpse of a relationship which challenges the hedonistic concept in Israel's theology appears in the story of Noah. The writer interprets the flood as a sign of God's angry condemnation of the world's wickedness. Because the earth was filled with violence mankind would be destroyed. Yet Noah and his family were spared. The rainbow appeared in the clouds as a token of God's promise never to repeat the catastrophe. The covenant with Noah's descendants was of God's free grace, and his mercy was unconditional (Gen. 6–9).

Further light on the mitigation of personal guilt comes in Abraham's encounter with God over the destruction of Sodom and Gomorrah. We have seen that the issue of the punishment of the innocent with the guilty was raised, but the story carries the argument beyond that problem. God is now challenged to save the many for the sake of the faithful few. In a kind of Dutch auction Abraham persuades God to agree that for the sake of ten righteous people he would spare the whole city of Sodom (Gen. 18.22–33). Here is a concept of reconciliation which entails a denial of strict retribution, and shows how a faithful few can shoulder a burden of guilt on behalf of the many.

The prophets in the eighth century BC, roared their denunciation of immorality and threatened terrible punishment for their wickedness; but the God they represented was not one who delighted in the dire consequences of wrong-doing. Indeed, the penalties could be withdrawn in response to amendment of life. In the case of Amos, for example, there were repeated threats in the words, 'I will not revoke the punishment' (Chs. 1–2). But the purpose of punishment was not mere vindictiveness: it had a disciplinary role. It could be revoked when the offender became penitent. If they did what was right, it might be that the Lord will be gracious (5.15).

Hosea had much to say about divine forgiveness. There are in his book warnings of the dire consequences of punishment, as for example: 'The Lord will punish their sins' (8.13), and 'Now they must bear their guilt' (10.2), but at the same time God could not bring himself to carry out those threats. 'How can I give you up? My heart recoils within me, my compassion grows warm and tender' (11.8). 'I will heal their faithlessness and love them freely' (14.4). The tension between justice and mercy is unresolved. In spite of the wickedness of the people there is hope of forgiveness and renewal. The pedagogic factor is unmistakable in divine punishment.

The same tension is to be found in the scriptures attributed to Isaiah of Jerusalem. Judgment is promised with an assurance which seems to leave no room for modification, still less for mercy. His message from God reads, 'I will vent my wrath on my enemies and avenge myself on my foes' (1.24). Yet in the very next verse there is the hope that a process of refining will be initiated. 'I will smelt away your dross as with lye and remove all your alloy' (1.25). As the fire of the smelter gets rid of impurities in precious metal, so the painful treatment which punishment entails will improve the character of those who endure it. To encounter the judgment of God is at the same time to encounter his love. Far from being vindictive, divine punishment is part of the saving activity of God.[4]

Jeremiah feels the same ambivalence as he predicts the punishment which will follow sin and at the same time sees the mercy of God shining through the gloom. The vessel which has been marred in the house of the potter can be re-made (18.1–4). The covenant with Yahweh has been breached, but another covenant will be made possible by an act of divine forgiveness. 'I will forgive their iniquity, and I will remember their sin no more' (31.34). The conflict in the heart of God is clear when he says through the prophet: 'I will chasten you in just measure, and I will be no means leave you unpunished' (30.11), and almost in the same breath: 'I will have compassion' (30.18).

Ezekiel is often accused of proclaiming the punishment of the individual wrong-doer as inevitable and automatic. 'The soul that sins shall die' (18.4). This is a mistaken idea. To quote the words of Paul Joyce, 'Ezekiel is not saying that particular individuals will be judged in isolation from their contemporaries. He is concerned about the House of Israel in a national crisis. They were not to blame their ancestors. . . . If they repented they would *not* be punished for the nation's past sins. They were to turn and live.'[5]

The exile was a turning point in the history of Israel. Politically it was significant because it marked the end of her existence as a sovereign state. During the period of the monarchy the various kings had failed to be true representatives of God in administering justice. The fall of Jerusalem in the early years of the sixth century BC spelt the end of an era. Instead of being a kingdom Israel now exists as a religious community under the domination of a succession of imperial powers. How would the post-exilic regime develop the doctrine of punishment in relation to God's dealings with his chosen people and in the achievement of social harmony?

In the first place there are some interesting features from the period of the exile which indicate how the exiles endured punishment at the hands of their captors. Instead of imposing penal sanctions on individual offenders in a political setting the covenant people were under the domination of hostile powers. Not only did they suffer persecution, but they were not sure that they would survive to return to their own land.

In Babylon King Nebuchadnezzar set up a golden image of himself, and commanded all the state officials, including justices and magistrates, to be present at the dedication ceremony and to fall down and worship it. Any who refused to do this would be cast into the burning furnace. Three officials, Shadrach, Meshach and Abednego, defied the command, believing that their own God would deliver them from this awful fate. They were bound and cast into the furnace, which had been made extra hot. They survived, and their executioners perished in the flames (Dan. 3).[6] The story was used to encourage those who were victims of persecution to stand fast in the faith of their own God. There is no record that burning in a furnace was used in Israel during the monarchy (but cf. Gen. 38.24).

Another form of capital punishment was to be torn to pieces and devoured by wild animals. When Daniel defied the decree of Darius the Mede, which forbade the worship of any god save the emperor himself, he was thrown into a den of lions. Three times a day this loyal Israelite had prayed to his God, his windows open towards Jerusalem. While Daniel was in the lions' den Darius spent a sleepless night, but when morning came he found the victim alive and well. The Lord had shut the lions' mouths. This form of punishment had never been prescribed by the kings of Israel and Judah (Dan. 6).

Another story is set in the reign of Ahasuerus, emperor of Persia. It describes how two of his eunuchs were plotting his death, when one of the Jewish exiles, Mordecai, overheard them making their plans, and his adopted daughter, Esther, told the king. When the king had investigated and found the story true, the two eunuchs were both hanged on the gallows (Esth. 2.23). The king's chief minister, Haman, was plotting a massacre of all the Jewish exiles and had already erected a gallows on which to hang Mordecai when Esther revealed this plot also, so Haman was hanged on the very gallows he had prepared for Mordecai (7.10).

These stories show punishment in a different light from that which guided successive governments in Israel as they dealt with the miscreants in their own land. The Lord's people were loyal to their God and were at the receiving end of penal action. Is this an earnest of the time when the problem of the theologians would be not how to inflict punishment in the name of God, but how to bear persecution and undeserved adversity to his glory?

The return from exile was made possible by a decree of Cyrus, king of Persia, about the year 537 BC, enabling some Jews to return to Judah to rebuild the temple in Jerusalem. Eventually some 49,500 settled in their native land with Zerubbabel as civil governor and Jeshua as high priest. Then, in the reign of Arterxerxes, Nehemiah was given permission to join them in order to re-build the walls of the former capital city. As governor he dealt with a number of abuses in a vigorous manner (Neh. 2.5–8; 13.15–30).

King Arterxerxes gave a letter to Ezra, a man well versed in law and described as 'the scribe of the law of the God of heaven', and it was this document which provided the authority and the substance of a new penal system for the post-exilic community in Jerusalem. Here is an extract from that letter:

And you, Ezra, according to the wisdom of your God which is in your hand, appoint magistrates and judges who may judge all the people in the province beyond the river, all such as know the laws of the Lord your God; and those who do not know them, you shall teach. Whoever will not obey the law of your God and the law of the king, let judgment be strictly executed upon him, whether for death or for banishment or for confiscation of his goods or for imprisonment (Ezra 7.25–26).

The administration of justice in the post-exilic era was marked by a recognition of the principle that the major aim of legislation was to uphold the ritual of a religious community. There was a departure from the political system of the monarchy. Even though the laws were given by God there had been the orientation of a sovereign state. Now the emphasis was on preserving the worshipping society. Although Ezra had been given responsibility for securing a legal foundation for the new regime a large measure of authority was placed in the hands of the priests. The administration could now direct penal measures to the ritual of the temple.

The priests had been involved in law and order from very early times. They had functioned in the finding of guilt by casting lots, by taking oaths, and by declaring the will of God in times of crisis, but to be involved in creating laws for the people lodged immense power in their hands. The community's relationship with God was paramount and the law must have as its primary interest the proper ordering of divine worship. New legislation with appropriate penalties was published in the 'priestly code' which is contained in sections of the Pentateuch and especially in Leviticus.[7]

There is evidence that the elders, who traditionally had administered justice at the city gate, continued to function under the new regime. They were called upon to adjudicate in connection with men who had taken foreign wives, an indication that ritual purity and cultic fidelity, rather than criminal charges or torts, occupied their attention (Ezra 10.14). Ezekiel had occasion to rebuke the elders, not because of injustice in the courts, but because they were worshipping idols (Ezek. 14.1–5).

Some of the examples of the new bias in the priestly code and the penalties for disobedience may be mentioned. The first is that circumcision must be observed as a method of preserving Jewish identity, and failure to comply with this law becomes a criminal offence. In ancient times the cutting of the flesh of the foreskin was widely practised as a mark of the male's initiation as a full member of the tribe. The Philistines appear to have been an exception to the rule. The Jews switched the ceremony to the eighth day after birth, but when this took place is not clear. The priestly editor inserts an account of a divine injunction to Abraham that every male must be circumcised on the eighth day, and the penalty for not doing so was that he should be cut off from his people (Gen. 17.9–14). The phrase 'cut off' probably means excommunication.

Secondly, priestly legislation made the observance of the sabbath day another sign that Israel were God's elect people, and again severe penalties were attached to the breaking of the law:

> You shall keep the sabbath because it is holy for you; Every one who profanes it shall be put to death; whoever does any work on it, that soul shall be cut off from among his people (Ex. 31.14).

The law itself may go back to the Decalogue, but the drastic penalties prescribed for its breach would appear to be post-exilic.

Thirdly, stern measures were taken against unnatural sexual activities. The harsh penalties for such activities were designed to keep the Jewish people free from pagan practices. There was no argument as to why unnatural sexual relationships were morally wrong. The aim of the penalties was to purge their cult from heathen rites. Homosexual acts are forbidden in very definite terms:

> You shall not lie with a male as with a woman, it is an abomination (Lev. 18.22).

> If a man lies with a male as with a woman, both of them have committed an abomination; they shall be put to death, their blood is upon them (Lev.20.13).

To approach a woman to uncover her nakedness while she is in her menstrual uncleanness was forbidden (Lev. 18.19). The man and the woman involved in the affair are equally guilty and both shall be cut off from their people (Lev. 20.18). The punishment for incest is even more severe. For sexual intercourse with a mother-in-law both the man and the woman are to be burned with fire (Lev. 20.14).

The same penalty was to be inflicted upon the daughter of any priest if she profaned herself by playing the harlot, but there is no record of burning alive being practised in post-exilic times (Lev. 21.9).

Bestiality was condemned because in pagan ritual it was practised in order to establish union with a deity through sexual intercourse with a sacred animal, such as cattle, sheep or pigs, but not horses or mules. To lie with a beast was perversion and it carried the death penalty (Lev. 18.23; 20.15–16).

Child sacrifice was condemned because it also was associated with pagan religion:

> Any man who gives any of his children to Moloch shall be put to death, the people of the land shall stone him with stones. . . . If they do not put him to death, but hide their eyes from that man . . . I will cut them off from among their people (Lev. 20.1–5).

The law was equally severe on necromancy:

> A man or woman who is a medium or wizard shall be put to death; They shall be stoned with stones (Lev. 20.27).

This recital of post-exilic laws and penalties is given in order to illustrate the vigorous attempt of the priestly editor to maintain religious standards and the ritual of the temple. Stoning and burning may seem to have a great deal in common with earlier penalties, but the purpose is different. It is not automatic retribution or ineluctable vengeance. It has a disciplinary intent. Its aim is to preserve the religious worship which expressed a relationship with God, symbolized their existence as a chosen race and provided hope of deliverance from sin. In other words, the aim of punishment was reconciliation with God. Paradoxically the cultus had to be preserved by salutary penalties because it sought non-penal measures for overcoming sin.

Because post-exilic Israel was a religious community rather than an organized state, the chroniclers appear to be less interested in the punishment of law-breakers than in providing alternative methods of dealing with offenders. Very few data are available to indicate whether these savage penalties were actually inflicted. The paramount concern was how sacral observances could achieve a measure of reconciliation with God and ensure moral improvement.

In this connection the ritual of the Day of Atonement is a relevant phenomenon. On this day no work was to be done and all the people were expected to observe a solemn fast and bring their offerings, not so much to appease God but to confess and wipe out all the sins of the past year, whether known or unknown, and to resume a fellowship with God which sin had disrupted. To some worshippers the rites might have had a magical significance: to others doubtless they would be efficacious through symbolism (Lev. 16.34).

An important feature of the day was the ritual of the scapegoat, or the 'goat for Azazel' (Lev. 16). After one goat had been killed and its blood sprinkled on the mercy-seat and the altar as a sin offering, a second goat, which remained alive, became the centre of another ceremony. The priest laid both his hands on the head of this animal and confessed the sins of the people. All their transgressions and iniquities were put upon the goat, which was then led away into the wilderness.

The scapegoat would carry all their wrong-doings and on his release would deliver them to Azazel in a solitary land. The man who had led the goat away would then wash himself and his clothes before returning to camp. Very little is known about the origin of this symbolic act. Azazel is imagined as some demon who lives in the desert and is the source of all the evil which is being returned to him so that the people might once again be made clean. Whether the rite goes back to the wilderness days remains a mystery, but just as punishment has a symbolic value as showing in dramatic form that the offence is being repudiated by society, so the ceremony of loading the transgressions of the people on to a goat for removal to a solitary place might well have had a beneficial impact on the character of the worshipper.

Although the use of imprisonment was among the penalties available to Ezra in the post-exilic religious community, there is no evidence that it was adopted. In earlier times there had been detention on remand, mainly it would seem in someone's house. The man who was found gathering sticks on the sabbath day was put in custody until he was stoned (Num. 15.34). The prophet Micaiah who insisted on telling Ahab the truth about the outcome of a military campaign was ordered to be kept in prison and fed on bread and water until the king returned (I Kings 22.27). A member of the tribe of Dan who cursed God was put in custody by Moses until the will of the Lord should be declared (Lev. 24.12).

Jeremiah was detained on three occasions for speaking out against war and on one of these he was put in a pit or cistern and had to be pulled out with a rope (Jer. 38.1–13). A seer named Hanani rebuked Asa, king of Judah, and was put in the stocks in a prison (II Chron. 16.10). Other references to people confined in prisons seem to occur during Israel's confrontation with countries like Egypt, Assyria and Babylon. It is significant that prison sentences were unknown among the Israelites and that a sign of the spirit of God at work was that captives would be released and prison doors opened to those who were bound (Isa. 61.1).

In connection with the cities of refuge, however, there was provision for the involuntary man-slayer to remain in detention for a fixed term,[8] not only to allow the anger of the victim's family to abate, but maybe also that he might cleanse himself ritually. He would be freed on the death of the high priest. Did this mean that the high priest had taken upon himself the blood guilt for the inadvertent killing and its expiation? Was his death seen as a sacrifice for all involuntary offences committed during his period of office? Perhaps the detention in the city of refuge had expiatory significance. In any case it is stated that if the fugitive fled and was killed, the avenger would not be guilty (Num. 35.27–28).

As far as can be ascertained from the documents it appears that little attention was given to the punishment of offenders. One reason for this was probably that greater attention was given to the use of liturgy as a means of restoring a right relationship with God. The singing of penitential psalms in the temple services has to be understood in the light of the theory that to mend one's ways would allay the infliction of pain. If the purpose of punishment is to produce the fruits of repentance, it ceases to be necessary when penitence was already manifest. So the worshippers sang:

I acknowledged my sin to thee, and I did not hide my iniquity; I said, 'I will confess my transgressions to the Lord'; Then thou didst forgive the guilt of my sin (Ps. 32.5).

Have mercy on me, O God, according to thy steadfast love; according to thy abundant mercy blot out my transgressions. Wash me thoroughly from my iniquity and cleanse me from my sin (Ps. 51.1–2).

Another reason for the decrease in emphasis on the punishment of offenders may have been the deeper understanding of divine mercy and this was also the subject of psalm-singing in the temple. In one psalm they sang:

Bless the Lord . . . who forgives all your iniquity. . . . The Lord is merciful and gracious, slow to anger and abounding in steadfast love. He will not always chide, neither will he keep his anger for ever. . . . He does not deal with us according to our sins, nor requite us according to our iniquities. . . . As far as the east is from the west so far does he remove our transgressions from us (Ps. 103.1–12).

That God does not requite us according to our iniquities created one of the gigantic problems of post-exilic theology. The conventional view was that wrong-doing would be punished. Retribution was built into the natural order of things. Divine justice demanded it. There were those who said the wicked would surely suffer pain and adversity, while the righteous would enjoy prosperity, good health and long life. That this cycle could be upset by the cancellation of deserved penalty was a staggering discovery or a shocking revelation. How many of the worshippers in the temple understood the full implication of what they were singing is impossible to assess. In any case liturgy does not lend itself to scientific analysis. The mercy of God was extolled. The pre-existent Christ is Lord of the Old Testament as well as of the New.

The corollary to the forgiveness of the guilty was the suffering of the innocent. If pain and adversity came to the righteous and health and prosperity came to the wicked, what happens to the concept that retribution was a law of the universe? The exile had brought this dilemma into focus. Did Israel really deserve such humiliation? The undeniable facts of experience challenged the hitherto unquestioned theory. The suffering of the innocent was a problem to be grappled with along with that of the forgiveness of the guilty.

This was the enigma which became the subject of the book of Job and which the dramatist presented with literary skill and deep mystical understanding. The author's name is not known, but the scene of the drama is set in the patriarchal period in which a man called Job had become a proverbial figure by reason of the fortitude he had displayed in bearing intense suffering. It set out to demonstrate that suffering was not necessarily a punishment for sin. It challenged the orthodox view that pain and adversity were inevitably associated with guilt.

Job was shown to be a blameless and upright man, yet he lost his property and his family – oxen, asses, sheep and camels, servants, sons and daughters. He was stricken with disease, which might have been leprosy, a common sign of divine displeasure. Not only was he in intense pain, but he was also an outcast. His agony could not be regarded as a punishment, though his friends tried to convince him that it was. He was forced by the facts of experience to challenge the doctrine which posited an exact balance between merit and fortune. There was no concept of life after death. Vindication had to come during his lifetime on earth.

Job asks for an indictment under which he is being punished. He feels no need of retribution or discipline. There seems to be no justice in the universe. How could God allow an innocent man to suffer such pain? Some suffering may be regarded as chastening, but there must be a large residue of unexplained adversity.

The conclusion of the drama is that man cannot understand the ways of God. The Creator has supreme wisdom, knows what he is doing and should be trusted where his purpose is veiled. Satan, the adversary who has been permitted to put Job's fidelity to the test, has to agree with Yahweh that the candidate has passed with distinction. The lesson, presented with great sensitivity, is that love which depends on gifts is suspect, that piety which has to be bought by prosperity is disingenuous, that disinterested religion is a mark of maturity, and that man should love God for himself alone rather than for the benefits he bestows.

Can it be true that theology reaches a greater degree of maturity when the expectation of rewards and punishments according to merit is outgrown? The lesson from the experience of Job would seem to be that happiness is a state of mind which is independent of gifts of material goods, and that misery is not the inevitable result of punishment, for 'Stone walls do not a prison make, nor iron bars a cage.'

In her discussion of the problem of innocent suffering, Elizabeth Moberly says the Book of Job does not go far enough in explaining its significance. It rejects the equation theory, that we can only suffer for the wrong we have done, but it does not provide a theory to replace it. It is as though the reader has left a room lit by a candle and is approaching a door into a room lit by a brilliant chandelier, but the patriarch from Uz does not open that door. He creates possibilities but does not significantly develop them. The book is negative and preparatory – a protest against an inadequate doctrine.[9]

Elizabeth Moberly finds a clue by which to carry the argument a little further in a concept of the interdependence of persons. Human beings are bound up with each other in such a way that the possibility of hurting one another goes with the possibility of doing good to each other. A burden inflicted by others can become a burden borne for others. This interdependence of persons is bound up with the doctrine of the Trinity. Man was made in the image of God (Gen. 1.26), but he was made in the image of the triune God, not the Unitarian God. This implies social solidarity. It is the basis of reciprocity or mutuality. Vicariousness is an essential feature of existence. One person may suffer for the sins of others.[10]

A deep insight into this aspect of human experience was achieved by the unnamed writer during the Babylonian exile whose literary masterpieces are known as the Servant Songs, and are contained in the Book of Isaiah. The principle of vicarious suffering is set forth with dramatic skill in these verses:

> Surely he has borne our griefs and carried our sorrows;
> Yet we esteemed him stricken, smitten by God, and afflicted.
> But he was wounded for our transgressions,
> He was bruised for our iniquities;
> Upon him was the chastisement that made us whole,
> And with his stripes we are healed . . .
> The Lord has laid on him the iniquity of us all . . .
> Stricken for the transgression of my people . . .
> He bore the sin of many and made intercession for
> The transgressors (Isa. 53.4–12).

Scholars argue as to whether the servant so described is an individual or a group. Those who think it is an individual choose one of the following: Cyrus, Hezekiah, Isaiah, Uzziah, Jeremiah, Deutero-Isaiah, Zerubbabel or an anonymous figure. Those who opt for the group interpretation see the servant as the whole nation of Israel, the faithful remnant of Israelites who survived the exile, or the ideal Israel – the nation as God intends it to be. For the purpose of this study the vital issue is the principle of vicarious suffering: the identification of the sufferer is a peripheral matter.

The collective interpretation has a long history. It was suggested by Origen in the third century AD. It was supported in the late eighteenth century by the French socio-anthropological school, notably Schuster. It was strongly supported by H. Wheeler Robinson, who claimed that it alone did full justice to the portrait of the suffering servant.

That a tribe or nation had a unity of its own and was often designated by the name of some ancestor is a familiar feature of Old Testament literature. A community may be spoken of as if it were an individual. 'Israel my servant, Jacob, whom I have chosen' (Isa. 41.8), is a common way of referring to the race. When Israel suffered defeat and humiliation at the hands of the Babylonian armies it looked as if she was being punished for her sins. The prophets had threatened that defeat in battle and loss of nationhood would be the penalty deserved because of her iniquity. But the writer of the 'songs' suggests that she was actually bearing suffering for the sins of other nations. The servant of the Lord is bruised and battered, humiliated and ostracized, not because of his own guilt, but as an atoning sacrifice for the sins of mankind. By his stripes there is healing for others.[11]

The servant was made to suffer by the aggression of other nations, but the anguish which he endured was not to be understood as punishment for his own sins, nor to satisfy the claims of justice. It was designed to move the enemies to repentance. Israel bore the suffering which the others deserved. The servant bore the suffering caused by the guilt of others as a privilege and earned for himself the title 'servant of the Lord'.

It has been argued that the picture of the suffering servant is not to be seen as a piece of history, a biography or even an autobiography, for there is no proof that the overthrow of Jerusalem by Babylon is being described; and the alternative interpretation is to recognize a universal principle in the experience of the sufferer, whether it is real or imaginary. Perhaps the unique individual, able and willing to accept the vocation of the suffering servant, has not yet appeared. Perhaps we have here a picture of an ideal person, described as the suffering servant – his appearance so marred, beyond human semblance – as a demonstration that innocent and faithful people can accept the privilege of bearing the painful consequences of the wrong-doing of others.

Throughout the history of Israel there were doubtless individuals and groups willing to fulfil the role of the suffering servant as an alternative to coercive or even military resistance to evil. During the persecution directed against the Jews by Antiochus Epiphanes in the second century BC the two attitudes were present. Mattathias led an armed revolt against the oppressor: Eleazar meekly accepted the flogging which led to his death. The latter suffered terrible agony, but he left an heroic example and a glorious memory (I Macc. 2; II Macc. 6.18–31).

Two further reflections on the concept of punishment in post-exilic times deserve mention. The first has to do with the part played by the devil in the aetiology of evil. We have seen how the Israelites' ideas on crime and punishment were influenced by surrounding tribes and nations, so now we have to look at the way in which the religion of Persia affected Jewish thinking during and after the exile. The religion of Persia was Zoroastrianism and in its sacred book the *Avesta* the origin of evil is explained by the existence of an evil being, an adversary, who is co-eternal with God. Whether Zoroaster himself formulated this doctrine is in doubt, but it became the orthodox teaching of his followers. Their catechism tells them that there are two first principles, one the Creator (Ohrmazd) who is entirely good, and the Destroyer (Ahriman) who is all wickedness. One is on high in the light, the other down below in the darkness. The Evil One invades the world and brings death, disease and sin into it. Like a trapped beast he lashes about and his capacity for hurting God's creatures is enormous. The struggle between good and evil goes on in the invisible world, good and evil spirits – angels and demons – fighting one another in eternal combat.[12]

There are traces of Iranian theology in the Old Testament references to the origin of evil. Eve blamed the serpent who beguiled her (Gen. 3.13). Evil spirits came from the invisible world and seduced women, and their offspring corrupted the world (Gen. 6.1–7). Satan appears as the Adversary in the Book of Job (2.1–9). Zechariah saw Satan standing at the right hand of Joshua ready to accuse him (Zech. 3.1). The evil spirits who are hostile to Yahweh are referred to as the host of heaven, and they will eventually be gathered together as prisoners in a pit (Isa. 24.21–22).

In the apocalyptic writings of the Old Testament the angelic rulers of the world incited the Gentiles to attack the holy people of Israel, but this dualism was only for a short period. The forces of evil would be subdued and cast into a subterranean dungeon to await their final judgment. The significance of this interpretation is that evil is seen as something greater than human wickedness. Iranian dualism shifted some of the blame for evil and suffering by saying that man is in the grip of forces beyond his control. The conquest of human wickedness by means of earthly punishment was therefore doomed to failure. Cosmic evil needed supernatural power to overcome it, and the triumph of good over evil was assured only by the superior power of God.

The Zoroastrian religion also had something to say about the punishment of the wicked after death, which is the second of the two reflections worth mentioning. The subject is discussed by Zoroaster himself. He says that souls are tested in molten metal and fire, and the wicked will depart to enduring misery. The wise Lord would assuredly requite evil for evil. He goes on, 'Lasting torment shall there be for the man who cleaves to the lie. . . . The wicked will be afflicted with lasting torment, feeding on foul food in the house of the Lie' (Yasna 45.7; 51.14).

In Jewish apocalyptic literature of the post-exilic era there is a feeling out for the possibility of life after death. There had been faint suggestions in earlier times, as, for instance, when the witch of Endor tried to communicate with Samuel's spirit on behalf of Saul (I Sam. 28.8–19), but generally speaking there was a sense of hopelessness about departed souls, who were thought to be living a shadowy existence in Sheol, a kind of underground pit. Any requiting of wrongs or vindication of innocent sufferers had to be in this life or not at all.

Job asked wistfully, 'If a man die shall he live again?' He cried out confidently that his vindicator will at last stand upon the earth and he will see him (14.13–15; 19.25–6). The psalmist had a similar glimmer of hope when he could not believe that God would give him up to Sheol, but would receive him to glory (16.10; 73.24).

The apocalyptic writers were much more confident about the resurrection of the dead and the life of the world to come. If God was good, they reasoned, there must be a time of recompense beyond the grave. If God was just there must be a vindication of the righteous in a future life. In the post-exilic section of the book of Isaiah there is a bold statement, 'Thy dead shall live, their bodies shall rise' (26.19).[13] In the book of Daniel this hope is echoed:

Many of those who sleep in the dust of the earth shall awake, some to everlasting life and some to shame and everlasting contempt; . . . and those who turn man to righteousness shall shine like the stars for ever and ever (12.2–3).

Having reached the view that life after death was a reality, the later writers could proceed to describe the nemesis which would overtake the wicked and the guerdon which awaited the good. The influence of Zoroaster seems unmistakable when we consider the visions reported in the books of Enoch in the Apocrypha. This is supported by Stanley B. Frost, who says the accounts of heaven and hell as places of reward and punishment and the idea of judgment by fire can only have come from Iranian eschatology as transmitted by the Chaldeans.[14] The wicked will be utterly consumed. Their doom is irrevocable. Unrequited sinners will be in great torment.

In this literature it is difficult to find a real doctrine of forgiveness. The writers were not worried about the problem of divine mercy, for their God was not merciful. The good are good and the bad are bad, and only the sorting of one from the other remains to be done.

The earth shall give up those who sleep in it, and the dust those who rest there in silence. . . . Then the most high shall be seen on the judgment seat, and there shall be an end of all pity and petience. Judgment alone shall remain; requital' (II Esd. 7.32–34).

The best that the theodicy of post-exilic Israel could produce in the full flowering of faith in the resurrection from the dead was a scheme of future rewards and punishments in heaven and hell. Threats of punishment through natural phenomena had failed to deter offenders, retribution on a justice model had been shown to be inoperative on earth, chastisement with a view to controlling behaviour had produced despair. The only remaining option was the punishment of the wicked after death: a hell from which there was no escape.

The irony of the situation is that Zoroastrian theology underwent a dramatic change in its later eschatological teaching. It espoused the belief that there woud be a final release from hell and sinners would all be admitted to eternal bliss. The sea of molten metal would purge them from all remaining alloy of sin. After the final purgation the whole human race would enter paradise where they would rejoice for ever and ever.[15] This came too late to affect the theology of the Old Testament.

PART TWO

PUNISHMENT IN THE
NEW TESTAMENT

4 THE RADICAL ETHIC OF JESUS

The student who expects to find in the New Testament a blue-print to guide society in its quest for a satisfactory penal policy will surely be disappointed. Firm conclusions as to what a modern community should do with its law-breakers are not easy to come by. The Christian scriptures provide no infallible ready-reckoner for the guidance of a criminal court, no clear directions as to whether punishment is permissible in a Christian country, no precise advice as to what kinds of penalty are appropriate for particular offences.

It is sometimes assumed that a religion with love as its central theme will have no place at all for punishment and that the only line it can take is to abolish the whole system of criminal justice. On the other hand there are large numbers of people, including Christians, who would argue that a country which had no sanctions for the enforcement of its laws would simply be a paradise of thieves and scoundrels. The dilemma is not to be resolved by quoting 'proof-texts', but by a careful analysis of the principles involved.

When we say our civilization is Christian we are thinking of the historical process by which certain standards of morality and fair-play have come to be generally accepted among us, but we have also to recognize that pagan elements have continued to influence social policies. The concept of power in the political sense involved a union of pagan tradition and Christian principles. If church and state were one it was because Christians had compromised their faith and accommodated their standards to the requirements of the secular rulers. However closely the religious and the political aspects of the present civilization may co-operate, they must remain distinct.

It must be recognized, however, that many of the moral ideals which Christianity gave to the world are accepted by many people today without reference to their origin. We hear of philosophical or natural ethics based on reason and conscience and divorced from the dogmas of religious faith. Indeed, religious beliefs are judged and criticized by secular man according to his self-contained standards of morality. In a pluralist society, where only a minority of citizens profess Christianity, is there any place for biblical insights?

There can be no doubt that natural morality and the Christian ethic often coalesce. The average man recognizes and condemns atrocities in the name of his humanity. He may even influence the Christian understanding of God by his basic sense of right and wrong, for as W. Moberly has pointed out, 'What purports to be revealed must be morally convincing before it can be accepted as authentic.'[1] It was a believer in natural morality, J. S. Mill, who said, 'In the example and teaching of Jesus is to be seen natural morality at its most sublime. An unbeliever would be hard put to it to find a better translation of the rule of virtue from the abstract into the concrete than to endeavour so to live that Christ would approve our lives.'[2]

On the other hand there are elements in the ethic of Jesus which are obnoxious to the unbeliever. It may be self-evident that he was a moral genius, but his radical views and his unconventional behaviour may be a stumbling-block to those who reject the gospel. When he demands forgiveness of a wrong-doer not seven times but seventy times seven he goes beyond what is rational by human standards. Here is something distinct from philosophical ethics. Here is a divine authority. To quote N. H. G. Robinson:

> There is no moral logic which will justify unrestricted and unlimited love in this imperfect world, except the moral logic of Christian faith, which bids men love their enemies because God's love actively embraces all men in an incredible brotherhood, the good and the bad, the just and the unjust, and has established in the midst of things gone wrong a kingdom of peace and goodwill, a kingdom of life and love.'[3]

Looking to Jesus for insight on the subject of punishment we have first to consider the theology on which his ethical principles were based. Many of his sayings look ridiculous unless they are seen in relation to the nature and activity of God. For the Christian, morality has a definite religious foundation. The attitude of God to the wrong-doer provides the standard for human justice.

When Jesus told his disciples that they were to be perfect as their heavenly Father was perfect, he was providing a theological basis for human behaviour (Matt. 5.48), and he amplified the nature of that perfection when he said: 'Be merciful as your Father is merciful' (Luke 6.36).

The idea that God punished the wrong-doer and rewarded the virtuous person is strongly challenged in the teaching of Jesus as it is presented in the gospels. The basis of his radical ethic is that God is a father who loves his children even when they do wrong. He does not treat them according to what they deserve. Curiously enough there is an appeal to nature to support the doctrine, 'God makes his sun rise on the evil and the good and sends rain on the just and the unjust' (Matt. 5.45).

Such teaching was not entirely foreign to the Jews. As was seen in the Old Testament literature, they had for many years sung in their worship:

> The Lord is merciful and gracious, slow to anger and abounding in steadfast love. . . . He does not deal with us according to our sins, nor requite us according to our iniquities (Ps. 103.8–10).

Jesus illustrated this aspect of the divine character in a number of parables. The prodigal son returned home in rags, having squandered his inheritance in loose living, and the father welcomed him with open arms, uttering no word of reproach or recrimination. The elder brother was angry and refused to join the welcome-home party. He said he was more deserving of the feast than his profligate brother for all the years he had toiled on the farm. Such a view of the heart of God was the basis of the ethic of forgiveness (Luke 15).

The same revolutionary doctrine is promulgated in the parable of the labourers. Those who only worked one hour received the same wage as those who had toiled all day. It was not surprising that the workers who had borne the burden of the day in the scorching heat grumbled at the employer, but he replied, 'Am I not allowed to do what I choose with what belongs to me? Or do you begrudge my generosity?' (Matt. 20.1–6).

The good people who listened to these stories were shocked by this revolutionary preaching. They were more familiar with the message of doom proclaimed by their old prophets. They understood that God would condemn and punish the wicked. Positive discrimination in favour of the bad was an outrage to their moral sense. That God did not punish sinners according to their deserts was a disturbing doctrine.

Another illustration which was offensive was that of the Pharisee and the publican at prayer in the temple. The Pharisee stood up and boasted of his legal rectitude. He thanked God he was not like the sinners, extortioners, unjust, adulterers and tax-collectors. He fasted twice a week and tithed his income. The publican, on the other hand, beat his breast and cried, 'God be merciful to me a sinner.' It was the bad man rather than the good who received the commendation of God (Luke 18.1–14). To the chief priests and elders of the people Jesus said, 'The tax-collectors and harlots go into the kingdom of God before you' (Matt. 21.31).

Having grasped the character of the God who showed mercy to sinners Jesus was able to expound the ethic which flowed from it. How a Christian behaves towards his erring brother is determined by his understanding of a merciful God. The strenuous demands upon believers would seem crazy unless seen in the context of a relationship with a loving God. We are now in a position to examine the radical ethic as contained in the sermon on the mount.

The 'sermon' is a collection of sayings of Jesus which appear to have been given to his followers rather than to the multitude. Matthew has the law of Moses in mind and is showing a parallel between the old law and the new. These ethical precepts are, in some sense, to constitute the new law; and they are on a different level from the regulations codified in the Jewish law-book. In the place of external obedience with penalties for disobedience, there was a new relation between man and God, a new dimension of moral experience and a new dynamic for the achievement of virtue. The precepts of Christ opened up new vistas of unattainable and even inconceivable perfection.[4]

A hint of what the new approach involved appears in the comparison between the law of Moses and the expectation of Jesus regarding homicide:

> You have heard that it was said to the men of old, 'You shall not kill, and whoever kills shall be liable to judgement.' But I say to you that everyone who is angry with his brother shall be liable to judgment (Matt. 5.21–22).

The act of murder is a punishable offence, but murderous feelings are in a different category. The new law is based on an ideal which implies a mystical relationship between man and God for its realization.

In place of the *lex talionis*, which had been widely accepted in the ancient world as a distinct improvement on unrestricted personal revenge, Jesus advocated a policy of non-resistance:

> You have heard that it was said, 'An eye for an eye and a tooth for a tooth.' But I say to you, Do not resist one who is evil. But if any one strikes you on the right cheek, turn to him the other also; and if any one would sue you and take your coat, let him have your cloak as well; and if one forces you to go one mile, go with him two miles. Give to him who begs from you, and do not refuse him who would borrow from you (Matt. 5.38–42).

The injunction to love one's enemies and pray for one's persecutors presented a similar test of Christian love. Such radical teaching was bound to create problems for those who have to adjudicate in criminal courts and for the public who happen to be the victims of crime, and scholars have been assiduous in their efforts to bring it within the bounds of common sense and social realism. As it stands it seems like a recipe for anarchy. In a world which depends on sanctions for the maintenance of law and order it makes Christianity look ridiculous. There must be some way of getting round it.

Could it be that Jesus was thinking of an ideal state in which all was sweetness and light? He was expecting the kingdom of God to come immediately. Could it be that his demands related to some future era? If he was thinking of the passing away of the present world order, he might have been thinking of an interim period which would lead to the end of the world. It is suggested that we have here 'counsels of perfection', intended to apply, not to the present world, but to the kingdom of God which is still to come. It may be replied that the injunctions would be irrelevant, for there would be no evil to resist and no enemies to love. There is no hint that Jesus was asking people to postpone obedience to a future date. T. W. Manson was right when he pointed out that as far as the kingdom of God was concerned the emphasis had shifted from future consummation to present realization.[5] The demands of the sermon are for this imperfect world now.

Another way of toning down the radical ethic of Jesus was to emphasize that the sermon was addressed to the followers of Jesus and not to the public at large. T. W. Manson expresses this as follows, 'The sermon is addressed to disciples, not to mankind in general. It does not deal directly with the affairs of the world at large. . . . It is not saying: 'This is how men in general should live if they really want to

build the kingdom of God on earth', It is saying: 'This is how you who
are in the kingdom of God must live if your citizenship is to be a
reality.'[6]

This concept of a 'double standard', one expectation from the
Christian and another from the non-Christian, has provoked much
discussion. N. H. G. Robinson affirms that it is wrong to suggest that
there is one standard for Christians and another for the rest. He says,
'God makes his claim upon all.'[7] On the other hand he admits that
man needs the grace of God in order to meet the demands of Christ.
He agrees with Calvin that it is *utterly against human nature* to love those
who hate us, to repay their evil deeds with benefits, to return blessings
for reproaches. We 'look upon the image of God in them, which
cancels and effaces their transgressions, and with its beauty and
dignity allures us to love and embrace them.'[8]

Taken out of context and viewed in legalistic terms it may well be
utterly against human nature to practise the ethic of the sermon on
the mount. Yet the same demands are made in Luke's collection of
sayings, known as the sermon on the plain, and here we are told that
Jesus was addressing a great multitude of people who came to hear
him (Luke 6.17). Jesus pointed to a supernatural power which could
lift men above the divisive forces of fear and hatred. His message was
that fellowship with a God of love introduced a mystical element
which made radical demands relevant to the political sphere. He was
challenging the social order of his day with an ideal which could only
be realized in the context of a theology of grace.

When Peter asked Jesus how often his brother might sin against
him and be forgiven – Was seven times enough? – he was calculating
in legalistic terms. There may have been a rule which set this figure as
a reasonable limit. After all, if forgiveness gave the wrong-doer a
licence to go on offending, a line must be drawn somewhere. Jesus
replied, 'I do not say to you seven times, but seventy times seven.' He
told a parable: A king was settling accounts with his servants. One
owed him a large sum of money which he could not pay, so the king
ordered him to be sold, with his wife and children and all that he had,
and payment to be made. When he fell on his knees and asked for
more time to pay, the king forgave him the debt and released him.
When the servant came upon a mate who owed him a trifling sum, he
showed no mercy and had him put in prison. The king was angry and
said, 'Should not you have had mercy on your fellow-servant as I had
mercy on you?' (Matt. 18.23–35).

It could be claimed that parables are to be understood as highly coloured illustrations of a general principle, rather than as precise rules for particular situations. It is unwise to draw out of these stories a blue-print for social policy. It is accepted that Jesus commonly made use of Semitic hyperbole. In the saying about turning the other cheek, for example, it has been said that in Matthew's version the 'right' cheek was deliberately specified, for this would mean (if the assailant was right-handed) that the back of the hand was used, so that we are dealing with an insult rather than a vicious assault. It is true that the parable of the two debtors, like the saying about lending to anyone who asks for a loan, would play havoc with the monetary system of a modern state, but the message is not in dispute, namely that the ground for being merciful is the mercy of God himself.

When each item in a parable is taken literally the search for guidance on penal policy becomes more complicated. For example: the unforgiving debtor, who failed to show pity on his colleague, was delivered to the torturers till he should pay all his debt. This does not mean that the ethic of Jesus justifies torture. There is a similar anomaly in our Lord's comment on two incidents in Jewish history. One was the massacre by Pilate of a company of Galilean pilgrims who were offering sacrifices in the temple. Their death was not to be seen as a punishment for their sins.

The other referred to an accident in which eighteen workmen building aqueducts at the Pool of Siloam had been buried under some falling masonry. They were not the worst men in Jerusalem. But having assured his hearers that these two tragedies were not to be seen as punishment by God for these unfortunate victims, Jesus adds, 'Unless you repent you will all likewise perish' (Luke 13.1–9). In neither saying nor parable do we find rigid laws for the administration of justice in society at large. We have to admit a large area of relativity in a Christian penal policy, but every Christian is obliged to measure his own reactions to wrong-doers by the principle of non-resisting love, consulting moment by moment his neighbour's need.[9]

Not only did Jesus teach the ethic of love, but he practised it as well, and it brought him into conflict with the authorities of his day. His example in dealing with offenders was a reflection of what he believed to be God's method for overcoming evil. He offered forgiveness to sinners and fraternized with them as if he were turning a blind eye to their wickedness. There may have been traces of hyperbole and ambiguity in his utterances, but there was no mistaking the message of his behaviour. He was defying some of the most cherished conventions of his day.[10]

In Capernaum a paralyzed man was brought to him on a stretcher. Jesus said to him, 'My son, your sins are forgiven.' The scribes said, 'Who can forgive sins but God alone?' Jesus answered, 'The son of man has authority on earth to forgive sins.' The scribes saw this as blasphemy; but when the paralytic picked up his pallet and walked, the people said they had never seen anything like it before (Mark 2.1–12).

Jesus became known as the friend of sinners. After he had invited a tax-collector named Levi to be one of his disciples, he was invited to dine with him, and he sat at table along with a number of people of bad character. The scribes of the Pharisees disapproved of this policy. It was the custom for religious people to keep apart from loose livers. Far from avoiding sinners, Jesus sought them out. This was a new and revolutionary policy of dealing with offenders, and it had far-reaching effects on the history of penological thought (Mark 2.13–17).

Referring to this dinner which Jesus and his disciples shared with the outcasts of society, J. A. Findlay writes:

> Jesus did not call the publicans and sinners to repentance, he invited them to be with him; it was enough that they should be themselves and be with him. In Levi's house he must have looked round on the motley company and said to himself: 'It is all very good.' Not: 'How shall I do these people good?' He enjoyed men and women as they were and for their own sake. He *did* save them, but it was precisely because he appreciated them for their own sake and not as cases on which he could exercise spiritual surgery.[11]

Findlay proceeds to give another example of the way in which Jesus showed himself to be on the side of the wicked rather than the good. A business manager was accused of dishonest dealings and was ordered to turn in his account books. He knew he would be relieved of his post and would be unable to obtain another accountancy post. He was not strong enough to dig and he was ashamed to beg. He thought he might as well be hanged for a sheep as for a lamb, so he called in the customers who owed him money and reduced their debts by as much as twenty or fifty per cent, so that they would look after him when he was out of work. The master commended the unjust steward for his criminal act (Luke 16.1–13).

This is one of the most controversial stories in the gospels. Findlay observes that Luke has listed four possible morals to be drawn from it and that two of them do not fit and the other two are taken from other contexts. 'To what contortions of expository legerdemain have the commentators been forced in order to make this parable respectable,' he exclaims. Manson overcomes the enigma by suggesting that the intention of the parable was to warn the people that they too were in a similar fix. The day of reckoning was near, and if they had any sense they would take urgent steps to avoid the impending doom. Findlay concludes, 'Why not admit that Jesus admired a clever businessman, not because he was honest, but just because he had character, was alive and alert and could make up his mind quickly. Jesus seems to have admired shamelessness.' It was in his delight in vitality for its own sake, this unfastidious appreciation of common life and human nature in the raw, that Findlay came to see God manifest in the flesh.

The same acceptance of sinners is illustrated in the friendship which Jesus formed with Zacchaeus, the notorious tax-collector of Jericho, who was despised by all respectable people in the town. When Jesus passed that way the little scoundrel was hiding in the branches of a fig tree. The visitor asked him to come down and be his host for the day. He appears to have said nothing about traitors who supported Roman domination of the country or cheats who became rich through fraud, yet Zacchaeus said he would make fourfold restitution for money unlawfully acquired and give half his possessions to the poor (Luke 19.1–10).

When Jesus was having dinner with a Pharisee, a woman in the city who was a sinner came in and proceeded to wet his feet with her tears and wipe them with her hair, and then to kiss them and anoint them with ointment. The host thought Jesus would never have allowed this had he known that she was a sinner, but Jesus said she loved much because she had been forgiven much. The Pharisees were shocked by the company Jesus kept (Luke 7.36–50). The close relationship which Jesus had with Mary of Magdala, out of whom he was said to have cast seven devils, must have been equally scandalous to respectable people (Luke 8.2).

Jesus refused to condone the death penalty for a woman who had been proved guilty of adultery – caught in the very act. The scribes and the Pharisees thought they would put him to the test on this matter of enforcement of the law of Moses which stipulated that such an offence merited lapidation. To their amazement Jesus said, 'Let him that is without sin among you be the first to throw a stone at her.'

The accusers went away one by one, and Jesus said to the woman, 'I do not condemn you, go and do not sin again' (John 8.1–11).

These gospel records show that with sovereign authority Jesus transcended the law and demonstrated the grace of God in the forgiveness of sins. His practice, like his teaching, was based on his conception of God. He had not come to carry out punishment according to legal requirements or exact proper revenge, but to seek the lost, to redeem the ungodly and to reconcile sinners to God. He identified with sinners rather than with the righteous. Very early in his ministry, when in the synagogue at Nazareth he announced his mission, quoting from Isaiah's prophecy, he omitted the reference to 'the day of vengeance of our God'. He said he had come to proclaim release to the captives. He may not have been giving specific guidance to a given community about penal policy but it was clear that to lock people up did not fit in with his practice of identifying with sinners (Luke 4.18). Indeed in another place he declares that those who visit prisoners are visiting him (Matt. 25.39–40).

There has been much debate on the attitude of Jesus to the law.[12] He befriended lawbreakers and he broke the law himself.[13] Does this mean that he was an anarchist? Much depends on what he meant when he said he had come to fulfil the law and not to destroy it. Most people will agree that some laws are unjust, that they offend against what is known as natural morality. For the Christian, love is the fulfilment of the law. The dynamic for the guidance of behaviour for the follower of Jesus is to love God and one's neighbour. Jesus did not abolish law, he suggested a new attitude to it. With the right spirit you do not need legal sanctions, yet they can have educational value. Jesus suggested a new commandment – 'that you love one another, as I have loved you' (John 15.12).

It was in harmony with the policy of acceptance rather than condemnation that Jesus expected his followers not to judge or condemn others. In order to do this they had to cultivate the grace of humility. Jesus said, 'Learn from me, for I am gentle and lowly in heart' (Matt. 11.29). He identified with a little child. When asked who is the greatest in the kingdom of heaven, he called a child and put him in the midst of them and said, 'Unless you turn and become like children you will never enter the kingdom of heaven. Whoever humbles himself like this child is greatest in the kingdom of heaven' (Matt. 18.4). When mothers brought their children for him to bless them, the disciples were turning them away, but Jesus said, 'Let the children come to me and do not hinder them; for to such belongs the kingdom of heaven' (Matt. 19.13–15).

It was in the same spirit that Jesus identified with the slave. After the last supper he washed his disciples' feet and explained why he had performed this menial task. He said he had given them an example that they should do as he had done. A slave occupied the lowest place in the social order. Jesus made himself of no reputation and his followers were asked to stoop to this level.

Jesus identified with the poor. When he met a rich young ruler searching for fulness of life, he advised him to sell up and give everything to the poor. It was hard for a rich man to enter the kingdom of heaven, he said. There was the constant threat of burglary. Whatever security measures he adopted to protect his property, a strong man may violently take away his goods. You are immune from the machinations of the robber if you have nothing for him to steal. Jesus himself was penniless and homeless, and this ascetic role enabled him to identify with the deprived and dispossessed who often had good reason for breaking the law (Matt. 19.16–22; 6.19–20; Luke 11.22; 9.58).

Jesus identified with the martyr. 'Whoever would save his life shall lose it, and whoever loses his life for my sake will find it.' 'Be not anxious for your life.' Behind these sayings is the belief in divine providence, by which the Christian knows he will be protected from danger as long as God wants him to remain on the earth. He can love his neighbour and practise non-violence without fearing for his life. Here is another way in which the radical ethic of Jesus leans heavily on theology. The Christian ethic of non-resistance to evil differs from ordinary morality in that it presupposes a personal submission to a divine plan (Matt. 16.25; Luke 12.22).

Not only was Jesus unafraid to die, he positively chose to give his life for the policy he was pursuing. As soon as his disciples acknowledged that he was the Messiah he told them about the death he was to accomplish at Jerusalem. He had no doubt that a strategy of non-violence would lead to crucifixion. It was the will of God and he had accepted it during the temptations in the wilderness. He was prepared to die at the hands of his enemies rather than summon legions of angels to protect himself (Matt. 26.53).

The episode of the transfiguration is best understood as depicting the experience of Peter as he tried to come to terms with the impending passion. The two Old Testament characters who appeared in the vision, Moses and Elijah, whose deaths had never been verified, represented the two pillars of the Judaic system of law and punishment. Moses was the lawgiver, Elijah had slain the prophets of Baal. Peter wanted to keep the old system and accommodate it to the new strategy of Jesus, but the glory which shone from the face of his leader on Mount Hermon convinced him that Moses and Elijah were to have no booths and that he was to listen to Jesus only. It was hard for Peter to understand that evil could be overcome by sacrificial love (Matt. 17.1–8).

So Jesus carried his cross to Golgotha. Seen from the point of view of the authorities of his day, Jesus was a rebel. Religious leaders saw him as a blasphemer, and political rulers believed him to be a threat to the security of the empire. By his proclamation of divine mercy and his practice of forgiving sins and identifying with sinners he was challenging the authority of political power and disrupting the religious structures of his day, so he had to be eliminated. Imperial domination and the subjection of the weak by armed force were bound up with the philosophy of vengeance. It is not surprising that the political significance of his death is being recognized by revolutionaries all over the world today. The man who identified with the criminals was classed with them on Calvary. Liberation theology sees Jesus in the contemporary world as the champion of the oppressed, the poor, the despised, the outcasts, the abandoned, the captives and all who are the victims of injustice and political domination.

Crucifixion was the most degrading of all punishments. It took place outside the city where the outcasts belonged. This rebel had been dragged from one place to another, interrogated, buffeted, stripped and lashed, and, in the most outrageous miscarriage of justice, was crucified between two robbers, numbered with the transgressors, the victim of the crowning infamy of history. Hanging there in anguish he told the penitent thief he would be with him in paradise, and, wonder of wonders, as his life ebbed out he gasped a desperate prayer for the forgiveness of his enemies.

By his identifications with god-forsaken, sinful, alienated people, Jesus condemns all forms of political oppression. What the public regarded as the lowest of the low, and what secular authorities considered the deepest ignominy, Jesus raised to the place of highest honour. 'The glory of God does not shine in the crowns of the mighty,' writes Jurgen Moltmann, 'but on the face of the crucified Christ.'[14]

But Christianity is not content to honour Jesus as a martyr or praise him as a political rebel. The church affirms that he was divine as well as human, that he was of one substance with the Father, that those who had seen him had seen God (John 10.30; 14.9–11). The supreme question for the student of punishment is whether the teaching of Jesus has divine authority and whether the cross reveals the true character of God. There have always been sincere critics who found it impossible to believe that the character of God was manifest in the death of Jesus.

In a later publication Moltmann has expounded the theme of the 'crucified God' in the light of the dialectical principle. He takes a cue from Ernst Bloch, a humanist Marxist, and asks 'whether only like can grasp like, or whether the unlike would not be better adapted to do so?' Argument from analogy is not ruled out, but there is an equally powerful argument from opposites. Love is revealed in hatred, unity in strife. The divine being was manifested in godlessness. God's righteousness was shown in justifying the unjust, the grace of the Creator in pity for the damned.

'The people who recognised Jesus in his truth,' Moltmann goes on, 'were sinners not the devout, the unjust not the just – indeed the demons first of all, as they were cast out.'[15] The implication of this dialectical principle is that Christians must depart from the narrow, cliquey policy of 'like being drawn to like', and must make fellowship possible with people who are unlike themselves, strangers, people who are different, their enemies. 'Loving people like themselves is a matter of course (Matt. 5.43). Love for the enemy, the person who is different, is the opening for the sympathy which takes upon itself and endures the pain of difference and enmity, and which seeks for correspondence in contradiction'.[16]

The gospels express this truth in a much simpler way. They say that Jesus rose from the dead as a vindication of his divinity. The resurrection story is not without its difficulties, but the essential lesson is that the one who was raised was this condemned, crucified and abandoned man. The disciples had seen him die the death of a criminal in the most degrading circumstances, yet they worshipped him. Their veneration was not for the god who punishes criminals but for the God who was executed as a criminal. This psychological reversal was the major miracle of history.

The most sensational act of worship for the early church was the adoration of the lamb. The most inoffensive of all animals, which through the centuries had been the victim of Jewish sacrifices, symbolized the self-giving of the man of Nazareth who bled to death on the cross. The imagery dramatized the enthronement of meekness.

Can those who sang 'Worthy is the Lamb that was slain' be expected to have theories about the punishment of criminals when their worship was centred upon a crucified felon (Rev. 5.12)?

If Jesus identified himself with sinners and was executed as a criminal, what are the implications for his followers? When he told his disciples that he was to be killed in Jerusalem, he added, 'If any man would come after me, let him deny himself and take up his cross and follow me' (Matt. 16.24). The reference to taking up the cross would be readily understood, for cross-bearing criminals were not unknown in Palestine. According to Roman law crucifixion was not part of the general judicial system, but was used to eliminate political rebels. After the resurrection it would have a deeper significance for the followers of Jesus. It would indicate that they also must be ready for a criminal's end; and although they forsook him and fled, subsequent records show that they stood the test. James was killed by king Herod's sword and Peter was arrested and put in prison (Acts 12.3).

When Jesus said the son of Man must suffer, he meant not only himself but his disciples as well. The designation *Son of Man* is an ambiguous term. It is the term which Jesus often used when speaking of himself, but it has a corporate meaning as well. When it was used in the book of Daniel (7.13–22) it was defined as 'the Saints of the most high God'. As Manson says, 'The meaning can oscilate between the sacred community as a whole, and its head.'[17] The interpretation is associated with the idea of corporate personality or the solidarity of mankind. We are not only individuals with a separate life to live, we are so bound up with one another that one person can suffer on behalf of another. The death of Jesus affects all humanity. Peter understood this, 'Christ suffered for you, leaving you an example that you should follow in his steps' (I Peter 2.21).

The lesson of this discussion on the teaching, example and crucifixion of Jesus is that the founder of Christianity was on the receiving end of punishment. The gospels have little guidance to give to those whose responsibility it is to define and administer penal policies, but they indicate that to bear pain on behalf of others is more likely to turn miscreants from their evil ways. Jesus offers an alternative to punishment. His concern is not to mete out just penalties for wrong-doing or exact revenge for pain and loss inflicted on others, nor even to make offenders smart in order to teach them a lesson. His strategy is to bear the burden of sin and to transform character by absorbing the evil in order to redeem the person who is precious in God's sight.

5 PUNISHMENT ACCORDING TO ST PAUL

St Paul holds a prominent position in the development of theology and ethics among the early Christians. Although he was not one of the twelve apostles who were with Jesus in the days of his ministry in Palestine, his training as a Jew and his success as a missionary among the Gentiles placed him above his contemporaries, while the abundance of his writings provided some of the material from which the doctrines of the church were eventually to be woven.

An examination of his works reveals a lack of consistent analysis of the theories of punishment and of clear reporting of the penal practice of his day. This is not surprising when it is remembered that his converts belonged to a minority movement which was more concerned with saving souls than with social organization. On the other hand the biographical details provided by Luke and various passages in the Pauline epistles give some idea of the reflections of the graduate of the university of Tarsus who, though he professed to despise worldly wisdom, was no mean thinker.

The several aspects of this thinking may be arranged in respect of his conversion experience and its implications for the strategy of transforming a murderer into a saint;[1] then the theology of grace and forgiveness and its relation to the death of Christ on the cross; next his echoing of the radical ethic of Jesus and its bearing on discipline in the early church; and finally, Paul's experience of Roman justice as he encountered it in his missionary journeys.

Paul's initiation into the Christian church came about in a most dramatic way. He claims that he came face to face with Jesus on the road to Damascus. He was going to that city with murderous intent. As a Jew of deep conviction he was opposed to the new religious

movement which apeared to be challenging the cherished
monotheism of his ancestral faith and despising the laws which were
a vital part of his religion. Knowing that there were men and women
forming a Christian cell in Damascus he was on his way to arrest
them and bring them bound to Jerusalem (Acts 9.1–2). He admits
that he persecuted the church violently and tried to destroy it (Gal.
1.13).

Instead of capturing the Christians he became a Christian himself. A light shone upon him and he was struck to the ground. He
heard a voice asking why he was so bitter towards the followers of
Jesus. Paul believed it was Jesus himself who was speaking. 'It hurts
you to kick against the goads,' said the voice. His conversion was
sudden and complete. He had come face to face with the risen Lord
and he gave his whole life to the one he had been persecuting. A
dramatic conversion often has a pricking of the conscience and a
train of thought, whether conscious or unconscious, behind the
experience. What factors had prepared Saul of Tarsus for this
sudden change in his life-style (Acts 9.1–9)?

He himself provides the answer. By his own admission it was the
shock of seeing Stephen stoned to death outside the gate of the city of
Jerusalem (Acts 22.20). He was guarding the garments of those who
were throwing the stones and he was consenting to the martyrdom of
this brave Christian. The spectacle of a man being done to death as
a criminal for saying that Jesus would change the customs delivered
by Moses had seared his soul. The crowning blow was struck when
the dying victim of official hatred prayed for the forgiveness of his
enemies. Here was a poignant demonstration of an alternative to
punishment and a vivid contrast to the bitterness which had
nourished his own criminal design (Acts 7.60).

Blinded by the flashing light on the Damascus road, Saul was led
into the city and was without food and drink for three days. Another
remarkable thing happened. He was visited by one of the Christians
he had come to arrest. The man was called Ananias and he actually
called him 'brother'. In spite of the danger involved in associating
with a murderer, notwithstanding the resentment he might well
have felt towards an avowed enemy, this visitor was offering his
friendship in the name of Jesus. It might have been a trap to ensnare
the unsuspecting members of the Christian group, but Ananias had
taken the risk. It was upon the basis of these two experiences that
Paul built up an ethical structure on a strong theological foundation.

The contrast between his own hatred and this forgiving love was the bomb that shattered his conventional philosophy (Acts 9.10–19).

From the disciples of Jesus with whom he mixed in Damascus and later in Antioch the new convert began to learn of the principles which made Christianity different from Judaism. He came to believe that God was not a stern judge but a loving father, that salvation and fulness of life did not consist in keeping the laws and earning a reward, but rather in letting the love of God be shed abroad in the heart, and that fear of punishment was not the incentive to moral living, but 'faith working through love' (Gal. 5.6). It would seem that this belief, inspired by the unconditional love shown by fellow-Christians, tallied with his own mystical insight, for he was able to claim it as a direct revelation of Jesus Christ.

He became a preacher and an evangelist, showing the same zeal which had driven him to persecute the church. This brought hostility upon him, and he met with persecution and intrigue in Damascus, so that he had to escape from his enemies by being let down in a basket over the city wall at dead of night (II Cor. 11.32–33). When he moved to Jerusalem the Christians there were afraid of him and did not believe he was a genuine convert. Again there was a brave man willing to take the risk. Barnabas introduced him to the apostles and vouched for his integrity (Acts 9.26–27). He was no longer Saul the persecutor; he was Paul the missionary. His message was that the alienated and the immoral could be changed by divine grace. He had seen that grace in the dying prayer of Stephen, in the courage of Ananias and in the steadfast love of Barnabas.

From his own experience Paul came to understand that the only way to change the human heart from bad to good was through acceptance and forgiveness, rather than through condemnation and punishment. He humbly announced that he was the foremost of sinners, but had received mercy from God. 'Christ Jesus came into the world to save sinners,' (I Tim. 1.15–16); 'There is therefore no condemnation to those who are in Christ Jesus' (Rom. 8.1). Whether by direct revelation of God or through the infectious kindness of fellow believers Paul had attained a deep insight into the character of God and it was associated with what he saw in Jesus.

We now turn to the passages in his letters which link this experience of forgiveness with the death of Christ on the cross. All guilty feelings, all sense of failure to reach the required standard of moral living, all despair at ever being able to live in harmony with one's fellow-men, all fear of being for ever condemned as an outcast were overcome by God's grace and mercy. Paul exclaims in wonder and amazement,

Christ died for the ungodly (Rom. 5.6).

God shows his love for us in that while we were yet sinners Christ died for us (Rom. 5.8).

We preach Christ crucified (I Cor. 1.23).

Sinful creatures were treated as if they were good, and it was not an experience which could be earned – it was the gift of God, and it was through the cross that this experience had become a reality. He does not fully understand the mystery of grace, but the message he received by revelation and verified in his own experience was that 'Christ died for our sins' (I Cor. 15.23). How are we to understand the connection between the death of Christ and the Pauline doctrine of justification by faith?

He made one statement which has given rise to a great deal of controversy and it is necessary to consider it in some detail:

Christ Jesus, whom God put forward as an expiation by his blood, to be received by faith. This was to show God's righteousness, because in his divine forbearance he had passed over former sins: it was to prove at the present time that he himself is righteous and that he justifies him who has faith in Jesus (Rom. 3.25–26).

The use of the word 'expiation' (in the older versions – 'propitiation') has caused some theologians to think of the death of Jesus as a sacrifice to appease a deity who is outraged by man's sin and demands some sort of satisfaction before he can forgive sins. In heathen sacrifices it was customary for guilty men to appease the displeasure of their gods, and in Judaism the blood of bulls and goats had been offered for the sins of the people. It is not surprising, therefore, that some scholars understood Paul to mean that the blood of Jesus satisfied the claims of justice so that a pardon could be won for sinners. The theory assumes that sin deserves punishment as just retribution. It claims that God could not let the offender off, or he would be encouraging evil. Because Jesus bore the penalty God was able to forgive without violating the demands of justice.[2]

To base a theory of atonement on this verse and a similar one in the Johannine literature (I John 2.2) is precarious indeed, yet some of the fathers of the early centuries were persuaded that the penal substitution idea was intended by Paul and John. One of these doctrinal experts, Tertullian, gave theology a legal cast which influenced Christian thinking from the third century onward. This Carthaginian lawyer said it was absurd to expect forgiveness when penance had not been performed. A pardon had to be paid for: morality would be undermined if forgiveness was cheap.

Cyprian carried the argument a stage further when he said one person's merit could be transferred to another. By his death on the cross Jesus earned an excess of merit which was paid to God as compensation for the sins of mankind. It was, however, Anselm (1033–1109), Archbishop of Canterbury, who stressed the strict requirements of justice, as if God were a judge in a criminal court. Man stood accused of sin which demanded death. The inexorable demand of the law was that the penalty be inflicted. In order that God could forgive, it was necessary for Jesus to bear the penalty of sin on behalf of mankind.

It is recognized that one of the difficulties raised by this Latin type theory is that it separates God from Jesus. God is pictured as the stern judge demanding the just penalty: Jesus as the loving friend of sinners willing to take the rap in order to satisfy divine anger. It does not fit in with Paul's teaching to say that Christ was punished by God. Anselm tried to overcome the problem by saying that God himself provided the sacrifice which satisfied the judicial requirements and made forgiveness possible without making it cheap.

Luther based his theory of the atonement on a juridical basis. On the one hand there was the wrath of God and the divine curse; on the other the love of God and his blessing. The German reformer did not accept that Jesus was being punished by God. The sacrifice of Calvary was God's sacrifice. He was the sole author of man's redemption. Luther's followers seem to have misunderstood their leader's point of view. In particular Melanchthon and Osiander interpreted the death of Christ on the forensic theory, namely that the suffering endured by Christ on the cross was the just punishment due to man's sin. Those who believe are saved because the righteousness of Christ is imputed to them. A legalistic understanding of the atonement came to be regarded as Protestant orthodoxy.

Calvin's position was unambiguous. He had no doubt that Christ was punished for the sins of men. He wrote,

By the merits of his death Christ paid our debts due to God's righteousness and placated his wrath, redeeming us from the curse of death to which we were liable, bearing the punishment of our sin in his body, so that he might free us from it.[3]

Calvin maintained that Jesus experienced all the signs of an angry and avenging God, but he was unable to explain how the love of God could be harmonized with such a vicious demand.

The penal substitution theory finds little support in the teaching of Paul. The text on which it is based consists of only ten words in Greek. If expiation were central to Pauline theology there would surely have been more than a passing and fragmentary allusion to it. The wonder is not that forensic terms are used, but that they occupy so small a place. If the theory means that God made Jesus bear the punishment for man's sin it can hardly claim the full support of Paul.

In 1968 Dr F. W. Dillistone surveyed the various theories of the atonement and concluded that the attempts to interpret the death of Jesus by the aid of forensic metaphors had been discredited. 'No strictly penal theory of the atonement can be expected to carry conviction today. To appeal to a system outmoded or open to criticism is to bring the whole doctrine into disrepute.'[4]

What is this 'outmoded system'? It is the administration of justice on the basis of inevitable retribution, which was in operation when this penal substitution theory was embraced. It assumed that an appropriate penalty must be inflicted on the wrong-doer, and there was no way in which it could be avoided. That the pain inflicted served no useful purpose to the individual or society was of no consequence. According to the 'outmoded system' there were no mitigating circumstances. Madmen and children suffered the due penalty. The law had to take its course. Behind the system was the concept of free-will and the belief that breaking of the law was always a reflection of deliberate wickedness. Punishment was therefore inexorable.

The theological basis of this system was that vindictive justice was the primary element in the character of God. Among those who defended this view was Nicolas Malebranche (1638–1715), a French philosopher. He said God could only be good within the limits of his justice, which was retributive purely and simply. If this is his sole moral attribute it can be manifested in the punishment of the wicked, since it does not conflict with any opposing attribute such as mercy. As long as the wicked are suffering for their sins that is all that matters.[5]

During the same period a number of liberal Protestants asserted that such a view of punishment was incompatible with the kind of God in whom the attribute of goodness or love had absolute priority over all other attributes. Peter Sterry and Jeremiah White, for example, believed that love was the supreme divine attribute out of which all others grow and to which they must conform. They based their belief upon the Johannine conception that 'God is love' and it corresponded to their own feeling of compassion for the suffering of sinners. This kind of theological stance was unusual if not unique in the seventeenth century.[6]

Since then human justice has been modified in criminal courts throughout the world, and inexorable retribution has given way to an emphasis on the utilitarian view that whatever penalties are awarded to criminals they should have some value to society at large and the offender himself. This is an illustration of the way in which ethics may affect theology. This is what Dillistone means when he speaks of basing the doctrine of the atonement on an outmoded system. He goes on to say that the psychological insights of family life lead to the view that humanity needs to be healed and mended rather than condemned and punished. The analogy today should be with the suffering that a parent endures through identification with an erring member of the family. The suffering of Jesus was not to appease an angry God. On the contrary it expresses his love.

This emphasis has many supporters among theologians today. Demant has expressed the idea cogently in the words,

Forgiveness is an agony.[7]

H. R. Mackintosh makes a similar point:

Let the man be found who has undergone the shattering experience of pardoning some awful wrong to himself, still more to one beloved by him, and he will understand the miracle of Calvary better than all the theologians in the world.[8]

It is not appropriate in this context to discuss alternative theories of the atonement, except to say that Paul's insight into the meaning of Calvary is that the death of Jesus makes the supreme appeal of the love of God to the heart of sinful man. We have seen that the apostle was overwhelmed by the pardon he received as a murderer intent on putting Christians to death. In amazement he cries, 'He loved me and gave himself for me' (Gal. 2.20). By absorbing the violence of his assailants Jesus revealed the divine strategy for overcoming evil and reconciling sinners to God. He gave himself completely to the recovery of fellowship with guilty men. By pouring his sacrificial love into the hearts of his opponents he was stimulating an answering love in their hearts. The objective of transforming character, rather than satisfying the claims of an abstract quality called justice, makes moral sense, and it shows how Jesus kept close to the picture of the suffering servant of Deutero-Isaiah (Isa. 53).

The next area for exploration of the thinking of Paul has to do with the ethical implications of his experience of conversion. How did the gospel affect his own attitude to wrong-doers and his administration of the infant churches over which he exercised pastoral discipline? There seems to be little doubt that his emphasis had shifted from law enforcement to the moral dynamic of love. Behaviour problems had to be seen as reflecting inner feelings rather than outward observance of rules. Paul saw the necessity to probe behind particular acts of law-breaking to the disposition from which they sprang.

Those actions which were disruptive of community life he called 'works of the flesh'. They included immorality, impurity, licentiousness, idolatry, sorcery, enmity, strife, jealousy, anger, selfishness, party spirit, dissention, envy, drunkenness and carousing. On the other hand were the good actions which had their corresponding sentiments. These he called 'fruits of the spirit', namely love, joy, peace, patience, kindness, goodness, faithfulness, gentleness and self-control. The presence of these emotional factors was the driving force of character. Behaviour was not to be regulated by law and punishment. The healthy community is made up of people who love their neighbour, and they can only do this when their heart is filled with the love of God (Rom. 5.5).

Paul echoed the principle that Jesus had expounded about being perfect as God was perfect, which meant showing love to good and bad alike. The love which he describes as being operated in human relationships is none other than the love of God in the heart of man:

Love is patient and kind; love is not jealous or boastful; it is not arrogant or rude. Love does not insist on its own way; is not irritable or resentful; it does not rejoice at wrong, but rejoices in the right. Love bears all things, believes all things, hopes all things, endures all things. Love never ends (I Cor. 13.4–8).

Brought up in the Jewish faith he had been taught to respect the laws which governed the life of his people, but he now saw legalism as a kind of slavery. Since he had come into an experience of the transforming love of Christ he viewed the law as a hostile power. The way of legal righteousness which the law demanded did not lead to salvation. It antagonized him. It led him away from God and deeper into sin. So the law was an enemy from whose tyranny Christ had come to deliver man. The love which Paul now saw as divine could not be imprisoned in the categories of justice and merit. 'Christ redeemed us from the curse of the law,' he said (Gal. 3.13). As Gustaf Aulen has put it, 'The triumph of Christ is the dethronement of Law and the deliverance of man from bondage to it.'[9]
Paul lays great stress on his freedom from the law.

> You were called to freedom, brethren; only do not use your freedom as an opportunity for the flesh, but through love be servants of one another, for the whole law is fulfilled in one word, 'You shall love your neighbour as yourself' (Gal. 5. 13–14). 'If you are led by the spirit you are not under the law' (Gal. 5.18).

In place of rules Paul put the self-determination of free persons whose motivation was the love of God uniting them with one another in mutual concern. This method of overcoming selfishness dug up the roots from which it sprang. 'Let no one seek his own good, but the good of his neighbour' (I Cor. 10.24). Paul was careful not to say that a person becomes a Christian by loving his neighbour. On the contrary one needed to become a Christian in order to love one's neighbour with the kind of love which did not take account of evil, but was kind to the enemy as well as to the friend.

Deliverance from sin was not something which could be earned by good works. It was the gift of God's grace. The experience of communion with God came through the forgiveness of sins. Paul used the word 'justification' to indicate that a person was treated as if he were good. He wrote,

> We hold that a man is justified by faith apart from the works of the law (Rom. 3.28).
>
> We are justified by his grace as a gift (Rom. 3.24).
>
> A man is not justified by works of the law, but through faith in Jesus Christ (Gal. 2.16).

Paul's emphasis on forgiveness as a fundamental feature of the Christian message was shocking to many people and it caused much dissension in the early church. It has been criticized on the ground that it represents the abdication of ethics, and implies that as long as you have faith in Christ it does not matter how you behave.

The fact is that Paul had a great deal to say about behaviour, and, as he tried to show how love operated among believers, he issued what might be called a new ethical code. The Christian attitude to various moral challenges of the day had to be worked out. Moral standards regarding sexual behaviour had not been cancelled. Love had to be translated into specific requirements in the daily life of the converts. In human relationships the law was not abolished. A new attitude towards the law was needed. There is a difference between law imposed from without by a hostile authority, and law which is freely accepted without compulsion, other than the compulsion of love.

In his letters Paul lays down a number of injunctions which constitute a new ethical code for church members. They were not to take revenge on the person who insulted and injured them, and here he echoes some of the sayings of Jesus:

> Bless those who persecute you. . . . Live in harmony with one another, do not be haughty, but associate with the lowly, never be conceited. . . . Repay no one evil for evil . . . live peaceably with all . . . never avenge yourselves, but leave it to the wrath of God: for it is written: 'Vengeance is mine, I will repay, says the Lord.' If your enemy is hungry, feed him; if he is thirsty, give him drink; for by so doing you will heap burning coals upon his head. Do not be overcome by evil, but overcome evil with good (Rom. 12.14–21).

Now much of this passage is reproduced from the Old Testament. The affirmation that retribution is in the hands of God was prominent in the book of Deuteronomy and in some of the Psalms (Deut. 32.35; Ps. 94.1), while the reference to giving food and drink to the enemy is to Proverbs 25.21. Writing to the Thessalonians, Paul repeats the injunction not to repay evil for evil, but to do good to all and he re-affirms that God is an avenger (I Thess. 4.6; 5.15). They were to bear their sufferings patiently and their fortitude would bear fruit. The designs of their persecutors would be frustrated in the providence of God (I Thess. 2.14–16).

Paul had not severed himself completely from the laws of his ancestral faith. A similar accommodation was made when he came with Barnabas to the Council of Jerusalem to discuss how far they were departing from the custom of Moses. The minimum that must be retained was that the Christian would 'abstain from what had been sacrificed to idols, from blood and what is strangled, and from unchastity' (Acts 15.29). He also associated himself with four men who went into the temple to purify themselves and paid the expenses of their sacrifices, in order to show that he lived in observance of Jewish law. His teaching on freedom from the law had brought hostility from the Jews in various places, and he was obliged to demonstrate that he had not discarded morality and the conventions of his contemporaries entirely. History has shown that the regulations of the early church were actually collected in a book called 'The Didache of the Twelve Apostles' published in the second Century AD.[10]

Paul was faced with another problem on account of his teaching on freedom from the law. If lawbreaking were to go unpunished would not the offender feel that sin does not matter? Does not the offer of forgiveness lead to laxity in morals? The apostle had to deal with a group of libertines who posed the question, 'Are we to continue in sin that grace may abound?' To withdraw condemnation of immorality, to pardon all offences, to regard a person as good when he is not – is this not tantamount to encouraging people to do wrong in order to give greater scope to divine mercy and human tolerance? Paul's answer was,

> By no means. How can we who died to sin, still live with it? You must consider yourselves dead to sin and alive to God in Christ Jesus (Rom. 6.1–11).

Two factors need to be considered when answering the charge of antinomianism. The first is that there is a psychological mechanism by which a wrong-doer is unaware of his guilt until the fear of punishment is removed. As Frederic Greeves explained,

> God in his infinite mercy does not allow his children to see their true guilt before the Saviour is in their view. By knowing himself pardoned and restored man says at length without qualification or excuse, 'I am guilty'.[11]

Only when faced with boundless mercy is an offender capable of acknowledging his transgressions. Until that moment his attitude is one of furtiveness and hypocrisy.

The other factor is that reconciliation enables the wrong-doer to accept his lot without resentment, and removes from him those feelings of dissatisfaction and alienation which have been the cause of his delinquency. Where an offence is provoked by deprivation of some kind, then positive discrimination in favour of the offender, far from encouraging him to repeat the offence, may actually remove the desire to rebel. This has been ably expounded by John Oman,

> As enmity against God is primarily enmity against the lives he has appointed for us, because we insist on using them for other ends than his, so reconciliation to God is primarily reconciliation to our lives by seeking in them only his ends. The immediate significance is reconciliation to the discipline he appoints and the duty he demands.[12]

The desire to please the one you love and adore is a far greater incentive to moral discipline than the fear of punishment. Delivered from condemnation and accepted into a loving relationship the soul is cleansed from selfish motives, such as anger, revenge, self-pity and insecurity, which are the emotions on which evil feeds and grows fat. When one has been fighting the law and is then freed from its requirements, the result is more likely to be moral discipline rather than laxity. Paul might have agreed that neither Stephen nor Ananias gave him a licence to continue in sin.

The ethical problems of Paul's pastoral ministry included the personal immorality of those who had been converted from paganism. In Corinth he had to deal with a case of incest. A man was living with his father's wife. Whether the father was alive still and whether the wife was a pagan are not stated. What is revealed is that the offence was so bad that even the pagans would have condemned it. Paul's directions were that the case should be dealt with in solemn assembly. He rebuked them for waiting so long before taking action against the brother. They had been shown to be arrogant in their complacency. They must 'deliver the offender to Satan for the destruction of the flesh, that his spirit may be saved in the day of the Lord Jesus' (I Cor. 5.1–5).

It is not easy to determine what this sentence amounted to. Was it the death penalty? It was believed that Satan had the power of life and death in his hands, and there was the grim case of Ananias and Sapphira who were rebuked for fraud and deceit and immediately dropped down dead on the spot (Acts 5.1–10). Had this been a capital sentence would not Paul have used the word 'body' rather than 'flesh'? He was probably thinking in terms of the destruction of the corrupt sexual desires, so that the body could be purified, which would mean that the assembly was required to excommunicate him with a view to his recovery. There is a similar stress on pastoral discipline rather than retribution in the case of Hymenaeus and Alexander, who were also delivered to Satan that they might be taught not to blaspheme (I Tim. 1.20).

It is supposed that Paul is referring to the same case of incest in Corinth when he wrote his second letter to the church in that city. This is what he said,

> For such a one this punishment by the majority is enough; so that you should rather turn and forgive and comfort him, or he may be overwhelmed by excessive sorrow. So I beg you to re-affirm your love for him (II Cor. 2.6–8).

Paul explained later in that letter that his main concern was that the church should show its loyalty to him by the careful way in which they dealt with backsliding among the members.

There were several cases of disorderly conduct in the Churches over which Paul exercised pastoral supervision. He warned the Corinthian church to withdraw from any member who behaved in a disorderly manner, as a fornicator, a drunkard or an extortioner (I Cor. 5.11). The Thessalonians were advised to treat the lapsed as a brother and not as an enemy (I Thess. 3.14). At Philippi there were two women, Euodia and Syntyche, who were not friendly to each other; they were exhorted to remember that they were fellow Christians and the rest of the congregation must help them (Phil. 4.2). Timothy was asked to keep an eye on Hymenaeus and Philetus who were guilty of godless chatter and were upsetting others by heretical views on the resurrection (II Tim. 2.16–19). Alexander the copper-smith had done Paul a great deal of harm, but no action was to be taken against him (II Tim. 4.14–16). There were problems with church members who held the form of religion but denied its power, and with others who made their way into households to capture weak women who were burdened with sins and swayed by various impulses (II Tim. 3.5–6).

Paul was eager to show restraint in all these cases of discipline in the churches. He did not intend to be severe in his use of authority which he held for building up and not for tearing down. This is in contrast to the writer of the Epistle to the Hebrews, who declared,

> It is impossible to restore again to repentance those who have once been enlightened, who have tasted the heavenly gift, and have become partakers of the Holy Spirit, and have tasted the goodness of the word of God, and the powers of the age to come, if they then commit apostasy, since they crucify the Son of God on their own account and hold him up to contempt (Heb. 6.4–6).

This is a classic expression of a point which greatly influenced discipline in the early church. Rigorous church leaders would sometimes excommunicate erring members and there was no way back into the fold. For any grave sin, especially apostasy, after conversion and baptism, there was no second chance. Even during times of persecution those who renounced their faith would sometimes be excluded from the congregation for ever. It was out of the bitter controversy on this doctrine that the Catholic system of confession and penitence eventually emerged.[13]

Reformation theology allowed for the experience of forgiveness to be renewed each day. Luther used a touching illustration – God has laid over us the mantle of divine righteousness, but our feet still peep out from under it and the devil nips our exposed extremities. We do not have to become active in fighting the monster, but we draw our feet in under the mantle and allow God himself to protect us.[14]

Paul's experience as a pastor of the flock illustrates the dilemma which confronts all who have to deal with lapses among church members. The Corinthian assembly was criticized because it took no action when the rumours of a man's immorality had spread far and wide. It seemed as if they were turning a blind eye to the scandal and that they did not care. When the assembly took drastic action and expelled the offender, they were repudiating their profession of love for sinners. Compassion won in the end.

One attempt to resolve the dilemma is for the faithful remnant to bear upon their own hearts the weaknesses and failures of the members under their pastoral care. Just as Jesus endured the agony in Gethsemane when he sweated blood, and the bitter pangs of the crucifixion, so Paul travailed for the salvation of his race. He says he had great sorrow and unceasing anguish in his heart, and could wish that he were accursed and cut off from Christ for the sake of his kinsmen (Rom. 9.2–3). With like pathos he told the Galatians that he was again in travail until Christ was formed in them (4.19). He also told the Philippians that for the sake of Jesus he had suffered the loss of all things and counted them as refuse in order that he might gain Christ, know the power of his resurrection, and share in his sufferings, becoming like him in his death (Phil. 3.7–10). To bear the sins of the weak and the wicked is what Jesus meant by taking up the cross.

Finally we have to look at Paul's attitude to secular law enforcement and especially his experience of Roman justice. There is some evidence in his writings that he was trying to keep the Christians aloof from the evils of a hostile world. 'Come out from them and be separate from them, says the Lord, and touch nothing unclean' (II Cor. 6.17). Whether he was thinking of Christians marrying pagans or members of the church becoming entangled with civic administration is not clear. From early times the church has had to face the issue of how far it can become involved in politics, in criminal justice, or in commerce, where it is so easy to lower moral standards and become enmeshed in the impurities of the world.

Paul expresses surprise that one of the members of the church in Corinth has actually taken a brother Christian to a secular court (I Cor. 5.9–13; 6.1–8). He had warned them not to associate with immoral men. Criminals must be avoided at all costs. Revilers, drunkards and robbers must be shunned. Any disagreement they had with fellow-Christians should be settled within the fellowship and not before civil magistrates. There was great temptation in a hostile world for the church to become a minority group and a narrow sect that did not become involved in worldly affairs. The early expectation of the second coming of Jesus also affected the attitude of the church to society at large.

It can hardly be surprising, therefore, that the details of state organization, of national guards and local police, of judges and magistrates, and the principles upon which justice should be administered and punishment meted out find little place in Paul's writings. His main advice to the Christians was to submit to the imperial power (Rom. 13), and this will be discussed in the next chapter.

In his missionary journeys Paul had occasion to be grateful for the protection he received at the hands of the militia and the magistrates. His life was threatened time after time by Jewish agitators. In Lystra he was stoned and left for dead. In Corinth Gallio, the proconsul, shut the door against the accusers when he saw there was no criminal charge to consider. In Ephesus the town clerk told the mob that the courts were open if they wanted an adjudication on Paul's behaviour. In Jerusalem the Roman garrison rescued him and brought him to their barracks for his own protection. In Caesarea King Agrippa and his officials ruled that Paul had done nothing to deserve death or imprisonment. Had it not been for the intervention of Roman police and magistrates he would not have lived to tell the tale. This doubtless affected the apostle's attitude to the 'powers that be'.

On the other hand, like his master, he was eventually at the receiving end of this system of justice. In Philippi he shared the inner dungeon and the stocks with common thieves and murderers, until an earthquake shook the prison to its foundations. At midnight he sang praises to God and it was the jailer, rather than the prisoners, who was converted (Acts 16). Along with Silas Paul had been beaten with rods, but when they knew he was a Roman citizen the magistrates let them go.

Paul was in prison in Rome, where he was guarded by Roman soldiers. It was from here, it is believed, that he wrote some of his letters to the various churches he had helped to found. It was no hardship to be locked up, he said. 'Rejoice in the Lord always,' he advised the Philippians (4.4), and when he wrote to Timothy he declared, 'All who desire to live a godly life in Christ Jesus will be persecuted' (II Tim. 3.12).

Nothing is definitely known of his death. He was expecting to suffer execution at the hands of the Romans during the persecution which broke out under the emperor Nero. There is in fact a tradition from Clement of Rome onwards that he suffered martyrdom between AD 64 and 68. Like his master he was nearer to the criminals than the judges, and this must have some bearing on the Christian attitude to crime and punishment.

6 THE DILEMMA OF CHRISTIAN ETHICS

Although the study of punishment in the Bible has revealed considerable evidence for the rejection of penal measures for the creation of social harmony, we must now examine the case for the opposite view. The radical theories contained in the gospels and the Pauline letters are to be taken seriously, but so are the sentiments expressed in the same documents setting out the sterner side of the Christian witness which seem to contradict the conclusions of the radicals. It is useless to deny that fundamental inconsistencies emerge from scriptural evidence. One result of this dilemma is that Christian influence on penal policies has always been confused and often irrelevant.

Throughout the Bible period ethics have been closely related to theology. What people believed about God has affected their moral teaching about human behaviour. Because of the close tie between morality and religion, man's understanding of the divine strategy in creation and redemption has determined his treatment of criminals and his attitude to sinners. On the one hand there is the view that Christ's teaching on the fatherhood of God and the love for sinners demonstrated on Calvary is a genuine and complete revelation of the character of God; on the other there is the conviction that judgment, condemnation, punishment and violent resistance to evil reflect God's true nature.

For almost two thousand years the Christian community has lived with the paradox. The 1662 prayer book of the Church of England invited communicants to confess the sins which have *provoked most justly God's wrath and indignation*, and then to affirm that it is *the Lord's property always to have mercy*. Likewise evangelists have been filled with tenderness and compassion as they have offered grace to vile offenders and in the next breath have proclaimed damnation to the unrepentant. In both attitudes they are being true to the teaching of the Bible.

A number of the sayings of Jesus recorded in the gospels reflect the awful destiny which awaits the wicked. Any system of theology which ignores this element of Christian teaching can hardly claim credibility. The appeal to fear and the threat of punishment cry out for examination. In the public mind God is identified with the policeman rather than with the criminal. Here are some examples of the sayings of Jesus:

> The master will come on a day when the servant does not expect him and at an hour he does not know and will *punish* him and put him with the hypocrites; there men will weep and gnash their teeth (Matt. 24.50).

> Cast the worthless servant into the *outer darkness*; there men will weep and gnash their teeth (Matt. 25.30).

> What will the owner of the vineyard do? He will come and *destroy* the tenant and give the vineyard to others (Mark 12.8–9).

> These enemies of mine, who did not want me to reign over them, bring them here and *slay* them before me (Luke 19.27).

> When the householder has shut the door you will begin to knock; but he will say: 'I tell you I do not know where you come from. Depart from me all you workers of iniquity. There you will weep and gnash your teeth (Luke 13.26–28).

In one of the parables Jesus likens God to a judge. If the allusion is to a particular case of a court official it is a reflection on the state of justice in those days, for a certain widow appealed for her grievance to be heard and her plea was ignored. Because she persevered and even threatened violence, the judge finally agreed to settle her dispute. The moral of the story is that people should be importunate in their prayers. But Jesus also added a further lesson, 'And will not God vindicate his elect who cry to him day and night? I tell you he will vindicate them speedily' (Luke 18.1–8).

Paul says some harsh things about judgment, wrath and fury as he discusses God's reaction to human wickedness:

> The wrath of God is revealed from heaven against all ungodliness and wickedness of men who by their wickedness suppress the truth (Rom. 1.18).

By your hard and impenitent heart you are storing up wrath for yourselves on the day of wrath, when God's righteous judgment will be revealed. For he will render to every man according to his works. . . . To those who are factious and do not obey the truth, but obey wickedness, there will be wrath and fury. . . . There will be tribulation and distress for every human being who does evil (Rom. 2.5–9).

Because of immorality and impurity and covetousness, the wrath of God comes upon the sons of disobedience (Eph. 5.6).

The Jews killed Jesus and the prophets, and God's wrath has come upon them at last (I Thess. 2.16).

Even when Paul was exhorting the Roman Christians to repay no one evil for evil, a stance which reflected the love ethic of Jesus, he then quoted from the Old Testament the words, 'Vengeance is mine, I will repay, says the Lord' (Rom. 12.19; Deut. 32.35). There are those who take the view that the ethic of non-resistance to evil is only valid because there is the back-up of divine retribution. Human beings can practise the gentler virtues when they are sure that divine punishment will vindicate them in the long term. Or put in another way, the ethic of love needs the theology of wrath to make it effective.

This is the point of view expounded by Paul Ramsey, who writes, 'Jesus himself did not think that the gospel of love would be sufficient by itself to resolve the totality of evil in many life situations, or to defeat the demonic power of evil encompassing even those purely personal relationships which in themselves are often amenable to love's persuasion.'[1]

In support of his argument Ramsey quotes the views of another American scholar, John Knox,

The practice of Jesus' ethical teaching had, in his mind, nothing to do with bringing the kingdom to pass. God was going to do that – and he was going to do it almost at once. God was going to bring in the kingdom, and he was going to bring it with power. . . . Jesus, although he enjoined non-violence upon his followers, did not attribute non-violence to God. Only God's power would suffice to destroy the forces of wickedness. Coercion would be needed, but it would be God's coercion, not man's.[2]

Ramsey makes the following comment on Knox's theory,

We frequently hear it said that Jesus' call to the strenuous way of limitless love lays down a method for making all the world a kingdom of God and is to be responded to with this end in view. For Jesus, however, the reverse is the case: the kingdom of God was already effective in the present age, and for this reason he believed the strenuous teachings could be lived out.[3]

According to Ramsey, while Christians are practising the ethic of love, God would be destroying evil with righteous vengeance. He concludes that making the radical teachings of Jesus cover the whole ground of action necessary to restrain or eliminate evil was simply not the religious ethic of Jesus.[4] This attempt to overcome the dilemma is important because it expresses the view of many Christians in the world today. They think God is first and foremost a judge who wields the power of life and death, that his mercy is secondary, temporary and conditional, and that behind the tender pleading for penitence is the big stick to subdue the reprobate.

The suggestion that it is anthropomorphism of the worst possible kind to attribute to God emotional and irrational outbursts of temper is answered by the assertion that the wrath of God is not the same as anger in a human being. It refers to God's inevitable opposition to sin. It is not a mood but an attitude. God is not capricious and unpredictable, he is constant in rejecting immorality. If he forgives the sinner it must not be assumed that he approves the sin.

This point of view was expressed by Cranfield in a learned comment on the wrath of God. He argued that Paul did not mean a personal reaction of God, but 'some process or effect in the realm of objective facts – an inevitable process of cause and effect in a moral universe.' He refutes the suggestion that Paul was attributing to God 'the irrational passion of anger' and affirms that there is an anger which is thoroughly rational. Paul would not ascribe to God a capricious irrational rage. He was thinking rather of indignation against wickedness which is an aspect of goodness in a sinful world. It is the opposition to evil of one who is all-loving.

Cranfield goes on to explain that in the words, 'The wrath of God is revealed from heaven against all ungodliness and wickedness of men' (Rom. 1.18), Paul is not referring to some punishment which God has inflicted on man, but to the gospel in which the love of God was displayed on the cross. The preaching of the crucifixion is both the offer to man of a status of righteousness before God *and* the revelation of God's wrath against his sin. In the gospel the divine mercy and the divine judgment are inseparable from each other. The forgiveness offered to us is forgiveness without condoning, and this is so because mercy is not cheap or superficial, but costly. The wrath of God is only truly known when it is seen in its revelation in Gethsemane and on Golgotha.[5]

Defenders of the sterner side of the divine nature sometimes argue that the universe reveals a natural bent towards punishment of wrong-doing and reward for goodness, and they conclude that God's judgment is revealed in creation. If God is good he must have placed a bias towards goodness in the world he created. So retribution is to be seen in the natural order of the universe.

Paul used the analogy of natural law when he wrote:

> Whatsoever a man sows that he will also reap. For he who sows to his own flesh, will from the flesh reap corruption, but he who sows to the Spirit will from the Spirit reap eternal life (Gal. 6.7–10).

The lesson usually culled from nature's constancy is that punishment inevitably follows wrong-doing, and that the moral order is as reliable as the natural order. If the creator of the universe is good, his creation must reveal goodness and evil must finally be overcome.

It is an inescapable fact that nature shows violent moods. Earthquakes, hurricanes, thunder and lightning, volcanic eruptions, drought, flood, pestilence, wild animals, all combine to strike fear into the hearts of primitive peoples. How could they avoid the conclusion that God was revealed as a stern and punitive monster? Calamities and natural evils were interpreted as punitive acts of God. Even in more recent times people have shown an infantile understanding of God's relation to man. Some remarkable 'judgments of God upon the wicked' have been reported. John Duncalf, who had stolen a Bible, cursed himself and wished that his hands might rot off, *and they did*. In 1747 William Whiston told the Archbishop of Canterbury that a plague which was destroying cattle would stop if the English reformed their manners. A hundred years later Dean Farrar regarded venereal disease as a divinely ordained punishment for sexual immorality.[6]

Jesus refuted the view that the accident in connection with the tower of Siloam was a punishment on guilty men (Luke 13.4) and that blindness was a punishment for sin (John 9.1–3). Far from proving the doctrine of divine retribution, it is possible to turn the argument round and argue that the constancy of nature shows the unconditional love of the creator. God makes the sun to shine on the evil as well as the good. Nature takes the risk and treats good and bad alike. If mercy is grounded in the universe, then love must bear fruit in the end. Sowing love is sure to yield a harvest of love in due course (II Cor. 9.6).

It has been said that there is evidence of divine wrath and vengeance in history. When Israel was defeated in battle it was a sign of God's anger. Nations are said to rise and fall according to their moral standards. There is, however, much evidence to show that the suffering and humiliation inflicted on many lands was not necessarily the result of guilt. There is such a thing as innocent suffering. Adversity may not be a sign of retribution. A country may win a war and then be worse off than its defeated enemy. Theological tenets which contradict the moral experience of man are suspect. If there is a bias towards goodness in nature and history it is to be seen in the ultimate triumph of love.

The dilemma of Christian ethics becomes even more acute when we turn to the theology of vengeance as it is revealed in the biblical teaching on hell. Switching the searchlight from this life to the next the problem of the punishment of the wicked presents even deeper problems. If evil does not receive its just retribution on earth, can we confidently look for judgment and redress after death? Can the thinkers who maintain that God punishes the evil-doer fall back on a doctrine of hell? According to the nineteenth-century jurist, Fitz-james Stephen, they can:

> Though Christianity expresses the tender and charitable sentiments with passionate ardour, it has also a terrible side. Christian love is only for a time and on condition; it stops short at the gates of hell, and hell is an essential part of the whole Christian scheme.[7]

The difficulty confronting the theologian who tries to organize the evidence is that the Bible teaching on the subject uses the language of poetry rather than scientific analysis. The apocalyptic writers of the period 200 BC to AD 120 used material symbols to convey abstract truth. Inevitably, instead of submitting a reasoned statement, they related visions. In place of logical argument they painted a picture. The emotional appeal was more important to them than intellectual accuracy.

One source of confusion in the biblical evidence is the mixing of metaphors. In one quotation the penalty is described as 'outer darkness', where there will be weeping and gnashing of teeth (Matt. 8.12). In another place there is a grim allusion to the worm that shall not die (Isa. 66.24; Mark 9.47). Some commentators think the worms are to be taken literally, which means that at the general resurrection the wicked will have physical bodies. Others say the worms stand for 'vexation of mind'. But the most popular symbol for the pains of hell is 'eternal fire' or 'the fire that is never quenched' (Matt. 18.8–9). There is no point in asking how the worms can survive in the fire, or how fire and darkness can exist side by side, for this literature is not meant to be analysed on scientific lines.

The idea of hell appears to have originated in the refuse dump which was located in the Valley of Hinnom, situated to the south-west of Jerusalem. It had become notorious in Jewish history as a place of heathen sacrifice, in particular the offering of children to the god Moloch (Jer. 7.31–34). It later became the place of punishment for apostate Jews. The bodies of the slain mingled with the rubbish. The site became known as Gehenna. The fire which burnt the garbage was never quenched. So this became the symbol of hell and the key element was eternal fire.

The number of times the word is used is an indication of the prominence given to Gehenna in the concept of punishment in the hereafter. Jesus is reported as saying:

Whoever says, 'You fool' shall be liable to the Gehenna of fire (Matt. 5.22).

It is better for you to enter into life maimed than with two hands to go to hell to the unquenchable fire. . . . It is better for you to enter into life lame than with two feet to be thrown into hell. . . . It is better for you to enter the kingdom of God with one eye than with two eyes to be thrown into hell . . . where the fire is not quenched (Mark 9.43–48).

I will warn you whom to fear: fear him who, after he has killed, has power to cast you into Gehenna (Luke 12.5).

You serpents, you brood of vipers, how shall you escape being sentenced to Gehenna? (Matt. 23.33).

We have here a pictorial allusion to some dark fate which awaited the impenitent sinner after death, with fire as the main element. With this to work upon the theologians set to work to formulate a doctrine of punishment in the hereafter. It emerged that fire could symbolize three different objectives: torment, destruction and refinement. The result was that there are three doctrines of hell, determined by what the various scholars believed to be the truth about God. They are mutually exclusive. A choice has to be made. Alternatively the whole concept of punishment after death might be ignored.

Augustine of Hippo (354–430) expounded the doctrine of *eternal torment*. This asserts that the lost will be subjected to torture in the flames of hell for ever and ever. With amazing confidence the learned bishop proclaimed that there would be no escape for the victims because they would be unable to repent. They would be conscious of nothing but pain and misery. They would be receiving the just reward for their sins. They would be furnished with special bodies which could be tormented without being destroyed. They would suffer unspeakable anguish with no possibility of deliverance.

Augustine had no difficulty in finding scriptural support for the doctrine. In the parable of the last judgment the judge says to the wicked:

> Depart from me you cursed, into the eternal fire prepared for the devil and his angels. . . . They will go away into eternal punishment (Matt. 25.41–46).

Jude refers to certain angels who had been kept in chains in the nether gloom until the day of judgment and who would serve as an example by undergoing a punishment of eternal fire (Jude 6–7).

In the parable of Dives and Lazarus, the poor man was carried into Abraham's bosom, while the rich man was in torment in Hades. The latter called to Abraham to send Lazarus to dip the end of his finger in water to cool his tongue, for he was in anguish in the flame. Abraham replied that between the two places a great chasm had been fixed, so there was no possibility of traffic between them (Luke 16.19–31).

In the Book of Revelation, an example of apocalyptic literature, it is said that Satan, after having been bound for a thousand years, was released from prison, mustered his forces and they were all consumed by fire which came down from heaven. Then the devil, the beast and the false prophet were thrown into the lake of fire, and they will be tormented day and night for ever (Rev. 20.7–10). 'The beast and the false prophet were thrown into the lake of fire that burns with brimstone' (Rev. 19.20). Brimstone is mentioned in a number of places in this book. Isaiah said a burning place had been prepared for the Assyrians and the fire would be kindled by the breath of the Lord 'like a stream of brimstone' (30.33). One bishop argued that this was not only to make the fire burn more sharply but also 'to make it more loathsome, in order to grieve the sight, smell and taste of the wicked, which had been surfeited with vain pleasures.'[8]

Through the centuries voices have been raised in criticism of the doctrine and by the seventeenth century they became more confident. One line of attack had to do with the large number of people inhabiting Gehenna. Where was this place and was it big enough to contain such vast crowds? Various estimates were suggested. One was that the population would be one hundred billion per square mile. It was argued that the traditional place – inside the earth – could not possibly contain the enormous number of damned souls and their resurrection bodies. Besides, would there be enough combustible matter to provide eternal flames, and could it burn without air? A solution suggested was that the sun was the site of hell, for it was a million times greater than the earth and it was fiery and permanently so.[9]

Another concern was about the children. In days when infant mortality was extremely high it was supposed that dead babies represented at least fifty per cent of hell's population, for only those who had been baptized would have escaped, and Protestants and Catholics did not accept each other's baptism. However, in spite of Augustine, the Catholics later refused to damn unbaptized infants and put them in Limbo where they were not tormented. Protestants likewise came round to the view that unbaptized infants would not be tormented.[10]

There was also criticism of the theory because it made no allowance for degrees of guilt. Women who adorned themselves unduly received the same sentence as brutal felons. Jesus spoke of some offenders receiving few stripes and others many stripes, but the doctrine of perpetual anguish makes no provision for degrees of culpability. If every single sin deserved eternal punishment, then any one sin of a damned person will fill his eternal life with infinite pain and there would be no room for the punishment of his other sins.

Probably the main objection to the doctrine was the infinite duration of the sentence. It was argued that the Greek word which is translated 'eternal' does not mean of endless duration, but rather 'age-long', and various estimates have been submitted regarding a reasonable length of an age, one being five hundred years. Some have made concessions to compassion and admitted that there might be periods of cooling. The greatest weakness of the theory is that it makes no provision for repentance and amendment. Although it is taught in scripture, it was not until the fourth century that it was set out as a doctrine; and there are biblical references which support alternative theories.

The second attempt to interpret the fire symbolism in the punishment of the wicked after death was that it *destroyed completely*. Instead of the effect of the flames being interminable pain it would be *annihilation*. The impenitent would cease to be. There was to be no immortality for those who failed to qualify for heaven. Their souls would *perish* in the conflagration.

The notion that the future punishment of the wicked would be the denial of immorality was enunciated by Arnobius, an African professor of philosophy, who became a Christian during the persecution under the emperor Diocletian at the beginning of the fourth century. He said what men feared most was corruptibility. To him perpetual life was the highest reward of faith and virtue, but it had to be won. The soul which failed to secure union with God in this life could not endure. Left to his natural state man would utterly perish. Earlier, Irenaeus, who became Bishop of Lyons in the year 177, had declared, 'He who has not recognized God deprives himself of continuance for ever.' Only the redeemed would enjoy immortality. The rest would be annihilated.

The following quotations show the support for this view in the New Testament:

> He will gather his wheat into the granary, but the chaff he will *burn* with unquenchable fire (Matt. 3.12).

> Fear him who can *destroy* both soul and body in Gehenna (Matt. 10.28).

> If the land bear thorns and thistles, it is worthless and near to being cursed: its end is to be *burned* (Heb. 6.8).

> Murderers, fornicators, sorcerers, idolaters and all liars, their lot shall be in the lake that burns with fire and brimstone, which is the second death (Rev. 21.8).

> The wages of sin is *death* (Rom. 6.23).

> He who sows to his own flesh will from the flesh reap corruption (Gal. 6.8).

The unrighteous, . . . like irrational animals, creatures of instinct; born to be caught and *killed*, will be *destroyed* (II Peter 2.9–12).

Unless you eat the flesh of the Son of Man and drink his blood you have *no life in you* (John 6.53).

The theory which was construed from these passages of scripture was considered less severe than that of eternal torment. To annihilate the wicked at death and allow only the just to be raised was seen as a mitigation of Augustine's doctrine and it was adopted in the sixteenth century by some Anabaptists and in the seventeenth century by some Socinians. The evidence regarding the Socinian view is confused, probably because there was no unanimity among them. It is thought that their leader, Fausto Socini, accepted the orthodox doctrine of eternal torment, but he also spoke of the natural mortality of man. There were certainly those among his followers who supported the doctrine of the annihilation of the wicked. That eternal life was a privilege of only the faithful made sense to Smaltius:

> It seems to involve extreme injustice if God gave man, whom he created mortal by nature, immortality merely in order that he should be eternally tormented.[11]

Conditional immortality has commended itself to some scholars on the ground that it is consistent with a process seen in nature. Evolutionists can understand how man has risen above the animals and by a positive response to the moral and spiritual challenge to have become immortal, whereas those who have set their faces against the stream of upward progress might well slip back into a kind of sub-human state which has no life apart from the earthly tabernacle.

Some defenders of the annihilation theory appeal to the law of atrophy, by which a faculty which is not used over a long period loses its ability to function. If a limb which is not exercised withers and dies, may it not be that a person who fails to deploy his power of spiritual perception eventually becomes incapable of communion with God? Another anology could be the death which comes to the branch of a tree when it is cut off from the trunk upon which it has depended for nourishment. Elizabeth Moberly has given a similar viewpoint.

> There must be a possibility of ultimate intransigence and moral deterioration. Hell is a corollary of the nature of wrong and the

intrinsic outworking of wrong-doing. Sin is a self-destructive force. One is not condemned to hell: one chooses it. But it is not for us to state at what point a person refusing to repent is finally damned.[12]

Some of the critics who opposed the eternity of hell and supported the annihilation theory took a less drastic stance and said the wicked would suffer a long period of torment before being completely destroyed. One of those who supported a period of severe punishment before annihilation was Ernst Soner (1572–1612), an honoured Lutheran. His argument was that the wicked would survive death and God would punish them with finite torments graded according to their sins before he annihilated them. Various guesses were made as to how long the period of torment might be, and the estimates varied from fifty to a thousand years. This was a mitigation of eternal punishment and a concession to divine mercy and a sop to those who resisted any mitigation of the eternity of hell.

Although the annihilation theory modified the orthodox doctrine of Augustine, it also raised some difficulties. If personality has a spiritual quality, it partakes of the nature of God and would therefore be indestructible. There is a widespread conviction that the human soul is inherently immortal, as is evidenced by the belief in re-incarnation. It is also claimed that the concept of annihilation offends against the Christian belief in the value of the individual. It seems inconsistent with the love of God to say that he created millions of people so that a selected number may attain unending bliss while the rest are totally destroyed. Arnobius endured martyrdom in the happy assurance that he would attain immortality, but it is hard to believe that apostasy would have meant the extinction of his soul.

The third attempt to expound the fire imagery in biblical teaching lays emphasis on the *refining* function of burning. This affirms that whatever punishment is meted out to wrong-doers after death will be *remedial* in its purpose and will result in the ultimate salvation of all souls. One of its early exponents was Origen (185–250), a learned theologian of Alexandria, who himself endured torture and imprisonment for professing Christianity. He suggested that the most important thing about fire, when used as a symbol of punishment, was its *refining power*. It is believed that he was influenced by his teacher, Clement of Alexandria, who also proclaimed that all punishment inflicted by God must have the *redemption* of the offender as its aim.

Although Origen was branded as a heretic in later years, there are some who believe that in the first three centuries of the Christian era the concept of purgatorial punishment was far from unacceptable. In the writings of Gregory of Nyssa (331–395) the doctrine of universal salvation was expressed with unusual clarity and conviction. Far from being a heretic he was an honoured bishop and a worthy defender of the Christian faith. He used the illustration of the refining of precious metals:

> As gold with its alloy is put into the furnace so that its impurity may be burned away, so the soul with its sin is committed to the purgatorial fire until the spurious material alloy is consumed and the gold is refined.[13]

The purifying aspect of suffering is recognized in the New Testament:

> Every one will be salted with fire (Mark 9.49).

> Each man's work will become manifest for the Day will disclose it, because it will be revealed with fire, and the fire will test what sort of work each man has done. If any man's work is burned up, he will suffer loss, though he himself will be saved, but only as through fire (I Cor. 3.13–15).

> You may have to suffer various trials, so that the genuineness of your faith, more precious than gold, which though perishable is tested by fire (I Peter 1.6–7).

Origen interpreted the eternal fire as an element created within the soul by its own evil thoughts and deeds, but he also recognized another fire which produced restoration and health. It was this line of thinking which eventually led to the doctrine of Purgatory, which was approved by Pope Gregory the Great (c. 604) and defined by the Council of Trent. It refers to the state of Christians who have been baptized but have not reached perfection at the time of death. St Catherine of Genoa wrote:

> Sin and rust is the hindrance, and the fire burns the rust away, so that more and more the soul opens itself up to the divine inflowing.[14]

It is not easy to determine when fire is used for penal suffering and when it signifies the love of God.

Reformation theology, with its emphasis on grace rather than merit, left no place for reformatory discipline in the after life. It retained heaven and hell as the two possibilities. It saw no escape from hell. 'Abandon hope all who enter here,' was the legend over the gate of the inferno in Dante's dream. Is there any evidence in the New Testament to inspire hope that remedial punishment will produce repentance and lead to a transfer from hell to heaven, or is there a great gulf fixed so that no one can cross over?

Admittedly the scriptural evidence is not conclusive, but a few texts provide a glimmer of hope. In the parable of the lost sheep, the shepherd looks for the erring animal, not until he is tired or until darkness falls, but *'until he finds it'* (Luke 15.4). There are verses in Paul's letters which have a universal flavour:

> As in Adam all die, so also in Christ shall *all* be made alive (I Cor. 15.22).

> That at the name of Jesus *every* knee should bow, in heaven and on earth and *under the earth*, and every tongue confess that Jesus Christ is Lord (Phil. 2.10–11).

> And I, when I am lifted up from the earth, will draw *all* men to myself (John 12.32).

The principal argument for the theory of universal salvation is not a series of proof texts from the Bible, but an understanding of the character of God himself. If his grace and mercy are really boundless, can it be possible that any sinner will remain outside the scope of his saving embrace? Of course, given the notion of free-will, there must always be the option to persist in wickedness for ever, but it is also possible that the Creator would understand how the stubbornness of his own creatures could be overcome.

It has been suggested that the trump card of the universalist is that the perfect salvation of the believer is impossible apart from the salvation of all. The human race if an organic unity. The solidarity and interdependence, so vividly expressed in the primitive concept of corporate personality and the later doctrine of vicarious suffering, means that saints and sinners are bound together with unbreakable cords, so that the saved could not fully enjoy the bliss of heaven if they were haunted by a Christlike concern for the lost. Paul said he would even suffer the agony of hell for the sake of the people he loved (Rom. 9.3).

There have been times when this argument was turned around. It was said that the sight and sound of millions in anguish increased the happiness of the blessed. They appreciated their own good fortune when they saw the torments of the damned. To certain types of people the idea of universal salvation is shocking, because it means that Satan might become of equal status with the angel Gabriel, demons with the apostles, and prostitutes with the Virgin Mary. There are certainly subjective and emotional factors affecting conclusions in the argument.

What effect does the Christian preoccupation with hell have on the volume of crime in the general community? Again there are two points of view. Preachers have claimed that religion was the firm foundation of societies because the fear of eternal damnation restrained vice. To question the validity of hell was to encourage criminals to ply their trade with impunity, they said. Criminals alleged that priests had invented the doctrine of eternal torment in order to preserve order in the land. It was also hinted that more people were put off the church because of its irrational teaching on punishment in the hereafter.

In view of the precarious origin of the Gehenna idea and the confusion which has arisen when the poetic allusions to the underworld have been analysed by theologians, it is hard to reach any definite conclusions regarding punishment in the hereafter. The prestige of the church gains nothing from pretending to a certainty it does not possess. It is better to offer the peace and power of the gospel than to threaten with hell-fire. If Jesus descended into hell and preached to the spirits in prison, let no wrong-doer abandon hope (I Peter 3.19). We cannot measure the boundless grace of God nor the extent of his victory over evil.

We must now look at one more attempt to modify the radical ethic of Jesus and Paul. The principle of non-resistance to evil may be accepted as a virtue in personal situations, but the Christian citizen has a duty to respect the judicial system which orders his communal life. The law of the land has to be respected side by side with the moral demands of the gospel. The administration of justice is often regarded as something to be endured even when it is distasteful.

It is argued that Jesus had this in mind when he said:

Render to Caesar the things that are Caesar's, and to God the things that are God's (Mark 12.17).

This seems to suggest that there are two spheres of obedience, one sacred and one secular, and that they are to be regarded as separate and distinct compartments of life. But had Caesar any authority independently of God? Jesus told Pilate:

> You would have no power over me unless it had been given you from above (John 19.11).

Was Jesus tacitly accepting the authority of secular rulers even when they were condemning him to death? It may well be that in spite of a flagrant miscarriage of justice, the judicial system of the Roman empire was not invalidated. It is noted that Jesus refused to join the Zealots in their policy of overthrowing the foreign power, however oppressive it might be.

Paul also stressed the duty of obedience to the civil power. He had experienced the benefits of Roman protection during his journeys around the empire. To him the officers of the state were divinely ordained to assist the cause of Christ. It was to the Roman Christians that he gave his great defence of rulers and magistrates:

> Let every person be subject to the governing authorities. For there is no authority except from God, and those that exist have been instituted by God. Therefore he who resists the authorities resists what God has appointed. For rulers are not a terror to good conduct but to bad. Would you have no fear of him who is in authority? Then do what is good, and you will receive his approval, for he is God's servant for your good. But if you do wrong be afraid, for he does not bear the sword in vain: he is the servant of God to execute his wrath on the wrong-doer. Therefore one must be subject, not only to avoid God's wrath, but also for conscience sake (Rome. 13.1–5).

This seems to mean that the state has an absolute right to use whatever force it thinks necessary to resist evil. This has led theologians to concede that law as well as gospel serves the purpose of God. This is plainly expressed by Philip Watson:

> A community in which the lawless might act with impunity would not long remain a community. It would be reduced to anarchy; and under conditions of anarchy the opportunity of a free, full and happy life for every man can scarcely be said to exist. As long as the

possibility of lawlessness remains, so long must the state have its laws, with sanctions to enforce them as may be necessary.[15]

Those who accept this interpretation of the authority of the state claim that God is not only a saviour but also a governor, that secular rulers are subject to his authority and that politicians have a responsibility to maintain order in society so that the gospel can be preached and grace offered to the people. Paul said that God 'has endured the vessels of wrath made for destruction, in order to make known the riches of his glory for the vessels of mercy (Rom. 9.22).

The dilemma of Christian ethics is clearly seen in the relationship between church and state. In Romans 13 Paul teaches that each has a claim on Christian allegiance. Is there no way of resolving the paradox? How does a disciple of Jesus combine his gospel of love and forgiveness with a secular system of law and punishment?

One solution is to say that there is no contradiction between the two functions. This is the view which is adumbrated by Thielicke:

> In equipping the state with punitive power, God is actually expressing love, for in so doing he takes the weak, oppressed and persecuted under his wing. The judge punishes for love of neighbour, whom he must protect. Love is the same but it is expressed in different forms.[16]

Of course this places a limit on what can be tolerated in the penal practice of the state. If justice is to be an expression of Christian love there can be no room for torture or brutality. This has been expressed by Philip Watson:

> Justice must be employed, not as an independent principle alongside of love – for apart from love we do not know what justice is – but as a subordinate instrument of love in an evil world.[17]

Other views about the relationship between church and state are less sanguine. It is a fact of history that the state has sometimes been corrupt and far from being a vehicle for the expression of Christian love. Paul was critical of secular rulers when he urged the Christians in Corinth not to take their grievances to the imperial courts (I Cor. 6.1–7). And he accused the rulers of this age of ignorance when they crucified the Lord of glory (I Cor. 2.8). In times when earthly powers have been hostile to the church, Christians have felt compelled to practise civil disobedience and to echo the words of the apostles in Jerusalem, 'We must obey God rather than man' (Acts 5.29).

The impossibility of harmonizing the two spheres has led some to withdraw from any association with a corrupt world. Some Christians, like the monks and hermits of old, withdraw from involvement with the secular world, because they see no hope of improving it. We are living in a fallen world, they say, and as it is coming to an end anyway there is no point in trying to humanize justice. Prisoners of conscience in totalitarian countries are under no illusions about the nature of secular justice. To quote Thielicke again:

> The laws of politics and jurisprudence are alien laws; they are strange as far as the kingdom of God is concerned. I cannot make the state an end in itself. The Sermon on the Mount is a disturbing fire which keeps me constantly on the move.[18]

A brilliant explanation of Paul's attitude to civil magistrates has been submitted by G. B. Caird, who starts from the principle that the apostle was imbued with the Jewish idea of angelic powers behind the pagan world-order. His phrase 'principalities and powers' reflects this concept of the state as being associated with supernatural beings. A pagan nation has a delegated and derivative authority, and if it demands absolute obedience it takes on a demonic character. By his death on the cross Jesus reconciled the spiritual beings and brought them within the power of God's redemption. This kind of reasoning may seem complicated to the modern reader, but its conclusion is not remote from contemporary thinking. Caird asks this question:

> If the angelic beings who preside over the pagan world-order are capable of being reconciled to God, does not this require us to believe that institutions such as the state, in which human sin is organised in what Tillich has called 'a structure of evil', are also capable of redemption?[19]

This conclusion offers a rebuke to those of the pessimistic school who see no hope for the transformation of the systems of punishment in the modern world. The Christian's loyalty to the state comes second to his loyalty to Christ, but by the influence of the radical ethic of Jesus, expressed in his devoted followers, the secular penal administration may be brought progressively into harmony with Christ's teaching on love and forgiveness.

PART THREE
BIBLICAL INSIGHTS AND PENAL HISTORY

7 CRIMINAL RESPONSIBILITY

The relation between church and state raises acute problems in the field of criminal justice. The antagonism of earthly rulers to prophets and martyrs has shown how difficult it is for the religious and the secular to live with the tension which comes from divided loyalty. The purpose of this section of the study is to show the relevance of biblical insights to the modern world and to illustrate some of the ways in which Christian teaching can contribute to the penological debate.

We have acknowledged that the ethical principles which operated in the history of Israel were confused and sometimes contradictory. The tribal practice of blood vengeance, the abortive attempt to devise a credible system of legal justice under the monarchy and the theological speculations of post-exilic Judaism reflected a variety of viewpoints which have persisted through the subsequent centuries, and, while they give no clear directions for legislators and judges in contemporary society, they cannot be completely disregarded. They form the background to the development of penal systems in the western world.

Christian literature enunciated revolutionary ideals which called in question the primitive customs of the ancient world. Its writers emphasized the revelation of the divine nature contained in the life, teaching and crucifixion of Jesus, together with the interpretation of the revelation by the early Christians, and put forward new insights into the purpose of God in the world. Here also there are anomalies and contradictions which make it difficult for ecclesiastical authorities to make specific judgments on how society should deal with deviants today. Yet the New Testament has thrown much light on the theory and practice of punishment through the ages.

Although the Christian has no blue-print for the penal systems of today, he has no mandate to shrink from commenting on the institutions of the state. His vocation demands that he offer some of the biblical insights which he thinks may illuminate discussion on one of the world's most intractable problems. The lack of dogmatism in biblical ethics serves to keep him humble, so that, along with representatives of other disciplines, he remembers that he is on a journey of discovery.

There are, of course, travellers who do not relish the company of the Bible student. They think religion has no place in debate. They view the state as having its own inherent laws. They may support secularization or they may have an ideology which precludes any supernatural orientation in social organization. They may have closed their minds to the very idea of theological interference, but it is more likely that even non-Christians will welcome theological comments if they echo the principles of natural morality.

Conversely there are Christians who refuse to participate in political debate. For them, matters of state are profane and beyond the brief of ecclesiastical authority. Like the monks of old they conceal themselves in the ghetto of private worship and closeted prayer. By their own choice and conviction they divorce religion from politics.

There is a third option. The Christian citizen can warn and criticize the state on the basis of biblical teaching without making dogmatic assertions or claiming to have instant solutions. If he admits that he has no esoteric information and that he is not privy to the means by which a utopian dream might be realized, he may have a chance of being heard. There is every reason why he should declare that he does not expect too much from the attempt to administer justice, as long as he adds that he does not despair of the future. He can admit that he is not 'of the world' and must not be 'conformed to the world', but he should also affirm that his duty is to strive to change the world.

One aspect of judicial theory in which both religious and secular students have a common interest is that of criminal responsibility. Is the individual offender fully responsible for his wrong-doing or is the community to blame for the social conditions which conduce to crime? Upon the answer to this question hangs the kind of judicial system which a country adopts. In a court of law the first decision to be made is whether or not the accused person did in fact commit the offence of which he is accused. The second question to be asked is to what extent he was to blame for his wrong-doing. To decide the degree of the offender's culpability is very much more difficult than to establish that he has actually broken the law.

We have seen that in the Bible individual and corporate responsibility are held together as an antinomy. The individual is answerable for his crime, but society must share the blame. If punishment is prescribed for the offender, what is to be done about the community which may be equally culpable? In the Old Testament there was emphasis on tribal and family responisiblity when the wife and children of Achan were put to death for his defiance of the ban, and when the seven descendants of Saul were killed for his slaughter of the Gibeonites (Josh. 7.24–25; II Sam. 21.8–9). There was also the primitive notion that 'the sins of the fathers might be visited upon the children to the third and fourth generation' (Ex. 20.5). The ancient proverb about the fathers having eaten sour grapes and the children's teeth being set on edge (Jer. 31.29) expressed in dramatic form the principle of corporate responsibility.

Ezekiel repudiated the proverb and proclaimed that the individual wrong-doer was personally responsible for his own sin. At one time scholars believed there had been a development from an early stress on corporate responsibility to a belief that the person who committed the offence was alone the guilty party. It is now accepted that this theory misrepresents the truth. There were elements of individualism long before the exile and there was an emphasis on communal responsibility after the exile. As Paul Joyce has pointed out, 'Throughout Israel's history the complexities of the relationship between the individual and the group were for the most part recognized as clearly as they are today.'[1]

One aspect of communal responsibility, which is said to reduce the guilt of the individual offender, is the abuse of political power, especially the oppression of the weak by the strong. As long as there are exploited minorities the government cannot be exonerated from blame. Concern for the poor runs like a silken thread through the pages of the Old Testament. The rich and powerful were often accused of being criminal in their treatment of the deprived and the defenceless. Those in authority were frequently reminded of their obligation to rule with integrity. Indeed, there was more condemnation of the rulers than of the ruled.

When the Israelite tribes demanded a king they were warned what the result would be. According to one historian, the enthronement of a monarch would be sure to bring oppression and exploitation. He reported the prediction of Samuel that the king would confiscate their property, take a tenth of their produce, conscript them for national service and make them slaves. 'And in that day you will cry out because of your kings,' Samuel had concluded. The later prophets alleged that this prediction had been fulfilled. According to Professor John Barton:

> The pre-exilic prophets consistently spoke as though the ethical norms to which they were trying to recall the nation were despised and rejected by those in authority as leaders of the community. . . . The perversion of justice and the denial of rights to the weak and the poor are condemned throughout the Old Testament. The duty of the strong to support and protect the weak is stressed.[2]

Amos thundered his denunciations of those in power who took bribes and turned aside the needy who came to the courts for redress, turning justice to wormwood (5.7–12). Isaiah condemned those who were heroes at drinking wine but who acquitted the guilty for a bribe and deprived the innocent of his right (5.23). He urged the rulers to seek justice and correct oppression (1.17).

Jeremiah was vitriolic in his criticisms of the social conditions of his day. He said national security could only be attained if the people executed justice one with another, if they did not oppress the alien, the fatherless and the widow, or shed innocent blood (7.5–6). The nation was corrupt because the establishment was more interested in gaining wealth dishonestly than in helping the poor and needy (22.16–17). The lofty ideal of the 'just king' had become a façade for the abuse of power. There could be no general rule of law when equal justice and civil rights were withheld from the populace.

The school of thought which opposed the monarchy were able to show that one king after another had committed abominations. During his fifty-five year reign, for example, Manasseh had done things more wicked than the Amorites ever did. Far from enforcing good laws he had actually made Judah to sin (II Kings 21.2–16). The significance of these angry denunciations is that a number of offences by individuals are due to social conditions. This is not to deny that there are crimes against natural morality which are culpable, however corrupt the administration, but the burden of the prophetic message was that the abuse of power made a mockery of any attempt to regulate society by the infliction of pain on a rebellious citizen who is denied elementary rights.

In the New Testament the follower of Jesus is seen as an alien in an earthly kingdom. Jesus told them that the rulers of the Gentiles lorded it over them, and they were expected to offer obedience, but this was not to be the pattern of his kingdom (Matt. 20.25). The conflict between the demands of the state and those of Christ is described in the Epistle of James: 'Do you know that friendship with the world is enmity with God? Whoever makes himself a friend of the world makes himself an enemy of God' (4.4–5). Peter shows his readers how to escape from the corruption which is in the world because of passion (II Peter 1.4). Paul said worldly power stood in antipathy to the spirit of God and earthly rulers were doomed to pass away (Rom. 5.13).

It is generally recognized that there is a higher justice than that which is reflected in legislation. Any attempt to reflect ideal morality in a man-made legal system is tentative and precarious. For Jesus and for his followers love transcends the law. As T. E. Jessop put it:

Love blurs the distinction between right and wrong, at times ignores it, and always dethrones it from the highest place. It takes us away from the dominion of law.[3]

Since it is impossible to translate love into legal precepts the laws of the state represent a relative justice. The laws of any country are subject to change and they are never likely to reach perfection. Laws are dynamic rather than static. When we speak of an increasing crime rate we have to remember that the passing of new laws is one cause of the increase. For example, in America in one particular year half the criminals arrested were held for violation of legal precepts which were not crimes twenty-five years before, and seventy-six per cent of inmates of federal prisons had been committed for offences which were not crimes fifteen years previously.[4]

Conversely changes in the law might mean that people found guilty under one regime are cleared under another. In 1968 Richard Oerton, a solicitor, wrote a book with the significant title 'Who is the criminal?' When he began to write it, homosexual acts done in private between consenting adults were still crimes, but before he finished it such acts (with a few exceptions) became legal. This change in the law meant that some 500,000 men in this country ceased to be criminals, yet they did not change and neither did their behaviour. Oerton concludes his book with these words:

And so it seems to me that crime is not an isolated pocket of illness inside a healthy society, but only the symptom of an illness which affects society at large. The families and the surroundings which produce crime are different, not in kind, but only in degree, from the families and surroundings which do not. And I believe that if we are to deal effectively with the root causes of crime we must look at ourselves before we turn to look at criminals.[5]

In spite of the mitigation plea of the apostles that they 'must obey God rather than man' (Acts 5.29), the breaking of the law of the land is not to be encouraged. As William Temple alleged, 'Frequent breaches of the law, however conscientious, are disastrous to society, and if the 'objector' is to be truly conscientious he must have estimated as far as he can the harm which he does by weakening the authority of the law.'[6] It is also to be noted that much of Christ's criticism of the law was not so much directed to ordinary moral demands as to the traditions of the elders, which he regarded as artificial.

The scriptures recognize two further factors which made crime inevitable and reduced the guilt of the offender. One was the concept of demon possession. When evil spirits entered a person they caused him to misbehave. The cure was exorcism (Acts 19.13–16). Other methods for curbing the lawlessness of demoniacs were locking up in a dark room, putting them in chains (Mark 5.3–4), music (I Sam. 16.14–23), or the administration of herbal medicines. At one monastery the lunatics are said to have received ten lashes every day, not as punishment, but to drive out the evil spirits.[7]

In modern times the mitigating factor of insanity has been recognized in law. The case of Daniel McNaghten, who was charged with the murder of Sir Robert Peel's private secretary in 1843, led to the drawing up of the 'judges' rules' which provided that a murderer may be pronounced insane if he did not know that what he had done was wrong. McNaghten was declared to be insane and was sent to Bedlam and was transferred to Broadmoor in 1864 where he died a year later. The recognition of 'diminished responsibility' was a step forward in the humanizing of justice.[8]

The other factor which seemed to make crime inevitable was given the name 'original sin'. It states that there was a supernatural agency of evil which led Adam and Eve to take fruit from the forbidden tree in the garden, and this meant that every member of the human race was born with a corrupt nature, so that sin was woven into the very texture of his being. Here was a notion of corporate responsibility. By reason of the solidarity of mankind the sin of the first man produced a bias towards evil in all his descendants. By his constitution man is prone to behave selfishly, until by the grace of God and Christian training he becomes sociable. The implication of this theological insight was that no person is an island and that we all share the guilt of each offender.

The nineteenth century saw rapid strides in the investigation of the factors in society which are conducive to crime. Many people who were unable to subscribe to the dogmas of the church were prepared to accept the findings of science. Bible students have been interested to discover the extent to which criminologists have confirmed the findings of theologians. It is now established that human beings are not independent units, each responsible for his own behaviour. Social solidarity has to be recognized on scientific as well as theological grounds. Repentance and humility are to be cultivated in the whole community as much as in the individual offender.

Criminology owes a great deal to the Italian anthropologist, Cesare Lombroso (1836–1909), who tried to locate the cause of deviant behaviour in the physical constitution of the criminal. He measured the skulls and other physical features of thousands of prisoners in Italy, and he concluded that the law-breaker was a throw-back in the evolutionary process. He saw the prisoner not as a wicked person, but as a special type of being recognizable by his mental and physical traits. The unfortunate miscreant was born that way and was in no way morally responsible for his actions.[9]

The emphasis on heredity prompted scientists to study criminal families in order to show that criminality persisted in successive generations. In the USA, for example, Dugdale traced the ancestry of the Jukes family and reported that of the 3,000 individuals in nine generations forty per cent had been thieves, prostitutes or murderers, and practically none had earned an honest living.[10] In Germany, Lange made an intensive study of identical twins and concluded that a propensity to commit crime was innate in a large number of cases.[11] In the second half of the century, however, other theories came to the fore and heredity fell into the background.

The rise of sociology provided another field in which to discover factors to indicate diminished responsibility for individual crimes and increased social responsibility for the conditions which provoked them. There had been voices crying in the wilderness of social deprivation even in the dark ages. St Thomas Aquinas (1226–1274) had conceded that theft was excusable when prompted by desperate need. Robin Hood was a popular hero because he robbed the rich of their ill-gotten gains in order to feed the starving families among the exploited peasants. Thomas More said stealing would not be overcome by stern punishments but by removing injustices in the social system. Rousseau had urged the poor to rebel against their lot, for the government was the guilty party.[12]

By the 1870s the sociological school was in the ascendant as scientific research began to confirm what the Bible had asserted about the corruption of the world. Using the statistical method the sociologists produced evidence to show that the volume of crime was more closely related to such factors as poverty, unemployment, bad housing and overcrowding than to the punitive measures used by the courts to deter offenders. Distinguished scholars from various countries pooled their conclusions, and their verdict was that guilt lay at the door of the community which allowed social evils to exist rather than on the shoulders of the victims of oppression who were rebelling against injustice. The findings of the school were summarized by the Frenchman A. Lacassagne, who said in 1885 at an international congress in Rome, 'Societies have the criminals they deserve.'[13]

In more recent times similar indictments of the social systems which are denying elementary human rights have been made. In his book entitled *The Criminals we Deserve*, Henry Rhodes declared:

Mass production is something more than an industrial technique . . . we mass-produce criminals.[14]

He went on to allege that we created conditions which made the criminal a menace to our security, and then devised elaborate machinery to entrap and punish this abortion of our own fashioning. If criminal man is immoral, he said, society is more so.[15]

In the USA Frank Tannenbaum traced the shift in the allocation of blame from the offender to the community. The constitution of the state of North Carolina had affirmed that the pursuit of wrong-doing had proceeded from a perverse will brought about by the seductions of the evil one, but more recent theories of crime causation had attributed crime to social conditions. Sociologists were now saying that criminals were the products of the economic system and any given country had as much crime as it generated. Crime could only be reduced by changing the community. There was an inevitability akin to that in the theological doctrine of predestination. Any attack on crime had to be directed not against the delinquent but against the social organism.[16]

During the past few years there has been a debate between criminologists and theologians with a view to discovering a common policy for the modern penal system. Much attention was given to a statement made by the American Friends Service Committee, namely:

The construction of a just system of criminal justice in an unjust society is a contradiction in terms.

In a symposium published by the group judgments are made by both disciplines on similar lines. A theologian doubted whether the existing social order was worth defending. It was usually tied up with the interests of a particular class. Disobedience to the law might be a moral duty – a way of bringing creative moral criticism to bear on the social order.

A criminologist was equally frank. He argued that the credibility of the criminal justice system had been eroded in the eyes of ordinary men, that the corruption of political life through bribery was more important than the crimes of working-class youths, that electoral procedures did not guarantee wisdom and virtue in the government, and that a constant factor in history was the defectiveness of human justice. He also mentioned the slogan, 'What is the crime of robbing a bank compared with owning one.'[17]

Criminology has identified a number of factors in the community which tend to be crime-producing. The capitalist system with its inherent desire to make money by competitive tactics creates an atmosphere in which dishonesty thrives. Urbanization has drawn families into large, anonymous groups in which mutual concern can hardly exist. The effect of excessive drinking of alcohol on behaviour is well-known, yet large profits are made from its sale, and seductive advertisements proclaim that it is a desirable and needful commodity. Unemployment debases a person and makes him feel worthless, yet it is regarded by some as an important strategy for the profitability of business. We cling to various institutions and practices which bring benefits to one section of the community at the expense of another. But to punish the victim and to speak of justice is to make a mockery of language.

A society which tolerates the inequalities of its economic system is unlikely to have much success in subduing its rebels by penal measures. In fact progress in liberating oppressed groups has sometimes come about because of crime. The Tolpuddle martyrs were found guilty of secretly banding together to form a trade union, and they were sentenced to transportation. Today such unions are an accepted feature of industrial life. The use of civil disobedience to get rid of an anomaly is no more wicked than the use of violence to preserve the status quo and defend oppression. According to Durkheim crime is a normal phenomenon for the integration of all societies, for it acts as a stimulus for creating new rules and is an agent of socialization.[18]

A nation which rejoices in military victories and makes heroes of those who have killed in war is not likely to have much success in curbing private violence. The difference between lawful destruction of life and property on the one hand and unlawful killing and mindless vandalism on the other tends to become blurred. To maintain dual standards of behaviour for governments and for individuals does not smack of equal justice. Gentlemen who boast of their military success and their accumulated wealth beat the criminal hollow in the magnitude of their immoral exploits. As G. B. Shaw cynically concluded in his book *The Crime of Imprisonment*, 'The divine judgment would not be able to distinguish between the two predatory insects: the criminal and the gentleman.'[19]

On this matter of shared responsibility for criminal acts the present century has thrown up another series of hypotheses. Sigmund Freud stimulated the technique of digging into the depths of the unconscious to find the motivation of human behaviour and to lay bare some of the experiences of the individual delinquent which had provoked his anti-social behaviour. It has become clear that the seeds of deviant conduct were sown in the mind of a child in his early years. Judges and magistrates have been invited to consider some of the factors which constitute mitigating elements in the emotional development of the offender for which other people are responsible.

Towards the end of the nineteenth century Krafft-Ebing began to investigate 'symbolic stealing' and proceeded to show that some offenders were driven by an 'irresistible impulse'. He cited the case of a baker's apprentice who had stolen a lady's handkerchief. He was conscious of sexual desires but had never had the confidence to approach a female. Stealing girls' handkerchiefs had become a habit as a way of obtaining a sexual thrill. Penitently he confessed that there were over eighty cases to be taken into account. He claimed he was unable to resist the impulse. Cases of arson and even murder often had a sexual significance. Unconscious motivation was a factor which diminished culpability.[21] R. B. Cattell and Sir Gervais Rentoul[22] examined a number of cases which exhibited a similar mechanism.

Psychologists have provided a great stimulus to the scientific understanding of crime. In every human being there is a conflict between emotional drives which are largely selfish and anti-social and the moral demands which require self-control and civilized living. In the absence of a happy emotional development to resolve this conflict there may well be a mysterious propulsion to break the law. The alternating personality is well known in terms of Stevenson's Dr Jekyl and Mr Hyde.

The search for causes of psychological disturbance has yielded some interesting results. One of the most constant factors in the aetiology of delinquency is defective family relationships. Uncertainty about one's parentage in the case of an adopted child, cover-up concerning the child born out of wedlock, the tension involved in living with a stepfather, stepmother or foster parents, the indignity of being placed in an institution, these sources of stress are often present in the background of a delinquent child. Parental quarrels, separation and divorce often bring divided loyalty and deep unhappiness to the offspring. Autobiographies and memoirs of ex-prisoners contain abundant material to indicate the origin of anti-social feelings in the victims of broken homes and disturbed family relationships.

Dr Grace Pailthorpe studied a hundred delinquent girls and found that half of them had been reared in an atmosphere where the ordinary love associated with family life was missing. She concluded:

Unwanted children experience little of the normal love of parents. This initial and most important stage in the child's development, if mis-managed, inevitably takes its toll.[23]

Ethel Mannin put it tersely:

If every child could have love in its life, there would be no need for prisons.[24]

A clinical study of a number of murderers was undertaken by the Swedish psychologist Andreas Bjerre, and he isolated a group whose main problem was that they had never become independent of their mothers. They had not been allowed to stand on their own feet. They were examples of the spoilt child syndrome. One of them, at the age of twenty-four, found a girl friend and when she became pregnant he murdered her. He had never been away from his mother and was afraid of responsibility. His sense of inferiority rendered him unfit for life's struggle. He said the prime cause of his misfortune was that he tried to escape from his mother's encircling arms.[25]

The attempt to trace the origin of anti-social conduct in a conflict between natural impulses and the requirements of conscience in the depths of the human heart has done a great deal to inspire crime-prevention techniques. Signs of maladjustment, such as nail-biting, tantrums, hysteria, night-terrors and enuresis, are indications that the help of a child-guidance clinic is required. The tragedy is, however, that even when parents know that their life-style is inimical to good behaviour in their children they are often unwilling or unable to make the necessary adjustment. There is a kind of inadequacy which is passed on by apprenticeship from one generation to another, and this is part of what theologians call the 'fall'. There is a kind of corruption in humanity which makes crime as inevitable as the cry of the cuckoo in the springtime.

Does this mean determinism? Has criminology led us into a trap similar to that reflected in the theology of Calvin? Is there no place in modern thinking for free will and personal responsibility? Has the corruption of the human race undermined morality? Are the concepts of evil, guilt and selfishness to be abolished along with witchcraft and demonology?

The answer is an emphatic negative. Even those who have been the most diligent in exposing the factors in social organization which generate crime have been vigorous in their defence of the notion of personal responsibility. One of the pioneers of criminological research, W. A. Bonger of Holland, was a convinced Marxist, yet he made it clear that in his view determinism did not mean fatalism. This quotation is worth noting:

> The reason for the persistence of indeterminism lies in the fear that, without free-will, morality would lose its foundation, that there would be an end to responsibility and that punishment would no longer be possible. This is entirely unfounded. Many determinists feel as responsible as anyone else for their actions.[26]

In her idea of interdependence, Elizabeth Moberly tries to keep the balance between individual and social responsibility which was a feature of biblical teaching.

> The wrong-doer may be responsible, but he is not solely responsible. That he is responsible still holds good. We have to consider the prior responsibility of other people. The wrong-doer represents only one side of a faulty relatedness. Don't blame one person only. Those who originated the faulty situation or rendered it intolerable are also blameworthy.[27]

It is necessary in the interests of truth to re-affirm the concept of the scriptures that individual and corporate responsibility are held together. The old proverb that 'the fathers have eaten sour grapes and the children's teeth are set on edge,' was repudiated not because it was untrue, but because it was misinterpreted. What was offensive about its application was that it sought to justify punishing children for the sins of their fathers. Its real meaning was that the behaviour of one person affects the behaviour of others, that wormwood and gall in one generation leave a bitter taste in the mouth of the next, and that the evils of society cast a blight over the individual.

The implication of this line of thought, which is expressed with great cogency in the words of Jesus, 'It is necessary that temptations come, but woe to the man by whom the temptation comes' (Matt. 18.7), is that social reform is an essential part of the just society. There can be no justice in the treatment of the individual criminal unless it is accompanied by an attack on the evils in society which contribute to the mass-production of crime.

8 THE PURPOSE OF PUNISHMENT

Many different attitudes to the punishment of wrong-doers have been delineated in the sacred books of Judaism and Christianity and these are to be traced also in the history of penal methods through subsequent years. Because of the variety of theories put forward to justify the infliction of pain on transgressors of the law there has been no consistent statement on the subject from theologians. The scriptural trumpet has given an uncertain sound and the battle has been delayed. The Christian church has had to live with this confusion and it is useless for it to pretend to a dogmatism which is unwarranted by the sacred writings on which her religion is largely based.

There is a sense, however, in which 'post-scriptural' revelation may go some way towards resolving its dilemmas and achieving a greater degree of clarity and unanimity in theological pronouncements on punishment. When Jesus promised the gift of the Holy Spirit he said there were many things he would have liked to say himself, but they would not be able to understand. But the 'Paraclete' would eventually guide them into all the truth (John 16.13). This further unfolding of divine truth would be in harmony with the biblical revelation but might yield deeper insight and clearer expression. New doctrines which deviated from the gospel would be heresies (Gal. 1.6–8). Nevertheless the church was undoubtedly encouraged to expect some of the anomalies of the written word to be resolved through the guidance of the Holy Spirit in subsequent generations.

Another factor which has to be taken into account is the place given to human reason in arriving at the truth. Christians differ in their evaluation of what is called 'natural theology'. Many of the moral questions which arise in everyday life are answered by means of common sense without reference to theology. It must also be recognized that a number of scientific discoveries have modified the teaching of the Bible. By the same token what professes to be a revelation of God in scripture is not necessarily accepted as authentic if it is manifestly offensive to one's moral judgment. There has to be some correspondence or interaction between divine revelation in the Bible and God's disclosure of truth in creation and human experience.

Such interaction is to be found in a comparison of scriptural teaching on punishment with the findings of scientific research. Truth is one whether it comes from the inspired writings of holy men centuries ago or through the application of human reason today, and confidence is increased when both channels of knowledge yield identical results. Are the discussions of philosophers able to throw any light on the aims of punishment? Can the scientists help the Christian to evaluate the teaching of the Bible? Is there any evidence that the 'spirit of truth' is guiding the church in its mission to provide moral leadership to contemporary society?

In order to answer these pertinent questions we have to examine the principles which motivated penalties for wrong-doing in biblical times and which have found philosophical expression in subsequent literature, and to show how theory has influenced practice in the punitive measures which have obtained in history. In an attempt to understand judicial procedures as they exist today we have to show how they have been influenced by rational thought and how far governments have modified instinctive drives and given logical reasons for their penal policies.

Those who have studied the customs of primitive tribes have stressed the instinctive basis of their treatment of deviants. They suggest that the origin of punishment is to be traced to the animal urge to retaliate when injured or threatened. The aim of impulsive reaction is to get rid of the interference. Even when the response is planned and deliberate the emotion of anger is still the driving force. The injured party is expected to defend himself by hitting back.

At one time retaliation was naked and unashamed, but with the advance of social organization some modification had to take place. The earliest function of law was to control this instinctive urge by specifying that the hitting back should relate to the seriousness of the original attack. We have seen that the *lex talionis* of Mosaic legislation was also embedded in the code of Hammurabi as early as 1700 BC.

Retaliation had to be kept within proper limits – 'an eye for an eye', not two eyes for one.

In ancient Israel there was a religious motive for punishment. Breaking tribal laws provoked the anger of the deity and might be requited by famine, pestilence or military defeat unless suitable punishment was inflicted on the offender. The murderer had to be executed in order to expiate the wrong he had done. Revenge was more than an instinctive reaction, it was a sacred religious duty. For the nomadic Israelites a precarious existence in the desert made the expiation of sin a major principle of penal action.

Philosophers who have examined this theory say that it reflects a natural craving in human beings to annul the wrong that has been done. A number of metaphors have been used to express the reasoning behind the notion that somehow punishment would annul the wrong. Punishment is an antidote to neutralize the poison, a debt that must be paid, a false step which has to be re-traced, a damage has been done and must be repaired, a false entry made in the record has to be expunged, a precedent has been set which must be cancelled, a stain has been received which must be washed out.[1]

Moberly refers to the institution of the duel, which used to be a popular method of wiping out an insult. In the eighteenth century, particularly in France, it was an accepted social convention in polite society that a 'gentleman' would wipe out an injury by killing or wounding his enemy. This is now seen as a piece of childish make-believe. It was artificial and ridiculous, for the death of an enemy does not really erase a wrong. Moberly concludes:

> Those who punish on high moral grounds are sure that they do so under some genuine moral obligation. In punishing a wrong-doer they intend, as far as in them lies, to cancel the wrong done. But to the critic, and often to the person punished, this sort of action, together with the whole order of ideas which inspires it, appears utterly inconsequent and irrational.[2]

Moberly agrees that the annulment theory has been supported by distinguished philosophers. Hegel explained that punishment was the turning back of crime against itself – 'the injury of an injury'. Bradley said that by punishment 'we annihilate the wrong and that is an end in itself.' Bosanquet argued that 'the principle of annulment is the ground and nature of punishment.'[3]

On the other hand George Bernard Shaw treated this theory with contempt:

> Human self-respect wants so desperately to have its sins washed away. . . . This is the real foundation of criminal law in human superstition . . . but what is done cannot be undone, and a man who steals must remain a thief until he becomes another man.[4]

Shaw went on to show that even when society has inflicted the punishment it still treats the criminal as a defaulter. He cites the case of Oscar Wilde, who thought that by the two years he had spent in prison he had settled accounts with the world and was entitled to begin again with a clean slate, but the world persisted in ostracizing him as if it had not punished him at all.[5]

Nevertheless the principle of annulment has been prominent in the philosophy of punishment the world over. In ancient Israel the outstanding attribute of the Creator was his righteousness. But this idea only came to the fore after the tribal deity was thought of as capricious, showing kindness one day and bad temper the next. The prophets proclaimed that God could be depended upon to do what was right. If he lashed out at the nation it was because they deserved it. Punishment was an aspect of his justice. Defeat in battle by Assyria or Babylon was seen as a natural consequence of their apostasy and wickedness. If God acted like this, then rulers should follow his example. Retribution became a major aim of penal practice. The infliction of pain on the offender was a way of wiping the slate clean.

This theological concept has been the basis of criminal justice ever since. In the Greek philosophy justice was one of the cardinal virtues. Socrates defined it as giving to each man what is *due* to him and the same idea is to be found in the writings of Aristotle. The Romans built their legal system upon it. In Britain the principle is illustrated in the statue of 'Justitia' on the dome of the Old Bailey in London. This gilded idol carries a pair of scales to show that British justice weighs the penalty against the wrong doing, and she is blindfolded to show that there is no partiality or discrimination. She carries a sword to show that the armed force of the state is geared to the punishment of wrong-doers according to their deserts.

The essence of the theory of retribution is that it is an end in itself that the guilty should suffer pain. The chief justification of penal action is that an offence has been committed which deserves punishment. Whether any benefit accrues from the action to the individual himself or to the community is of no consequence. No account is taken of the circumstances of the offence, the age of the accused or the state of mind of the offender. The punishment must fit the crime. The wrong-doer must get the just reward of his sins.[6]

The most famous of the protagonists of the theory of retribution was Immanuel Kant (1724–1804), the German philosopher, who wrote:

> Judicial punishment can never serve merely as a means to further another good, whether for the offender himself or society, but must always be inflicted on him for the sole reason that he has committed a crime. The law of punishment is a categorical imperative, and woe to him who crawls through the serpentine windings of the happiness theory seeking to discover something which in virtue of the benefit it promises will release him from the duty of punishment or even from a faction of its full severity.[7]

Those who defend Kant's theory say that it is based on intuition. They appeal to the sense of horror with which the average man looks at crime. There is a widespread feeling that the bad person should be punished and the good person rewarded. How can we say we live in a moral universe unless we get what we deserve? And the justification of the theory is that God administers the universe on the principle of retribution, for did not St Paul affirm that God 'would render to every man according to his works?' (Rom. 2.6).

Thomas Carlyle was a passionate supporter of the Kantian theory:

> Just hatred of scoundrels, I say, fixed, irreconcilable, inexorable enmity to the enemies of God, this and not love for them and incessant whitewashing and dressing and cockering of them must, if you look into it, be the backbone of any religion whatever. Revenge, my friends; revenge, and the natural hatred of scoundrels ... this is for ever a more intrinsically correct and even a divine feeling in the mind of every man. Only the excess of it is diabolic; the essence, I say, is man-like and even god-like – a monition sent to poor man by the Maker himself.[8]

Carlyle's emotional outburst displayed commendable honesty. He acknowledged that the theory was based on revenge and hatred of scoundrels. Other members of the school prefer to use the euphemism 'righteous indignation'. They say that an aversion from evil is essential if the distinction between right and wrong is to have any meaning. T. H. Green was less vehement in his explanation:

> Indignation against wrong done to another person has nothing in common with the desire to avenge a wrong done to one's self. It borrows the language of private revenge just as the love of God borrows the language of sensuous love.[9]

On the other hand, Ewing says there is a very thin line between righteous and unrighteous indignation, and he suggests that anger has little intrinsic value in guiding society in its attitude to criminals. He adds:

> It seems strange that a kind of action which under ordinary conditions is regarded as the very extreme of moral depravity should become a virtue in the case of punishment.[10]

The weakness of the theory of retribution is to be found in its attempt to equate the punishment inflicted with the crime committed. In order for the punishment to be 'just', all wrong-doing would have to be criminal, but the state cannot legislate against ingratitude, avarice and pride. Such dispositions are beyond the range of criminal law. Legislatures single out certain bad acts for special condemnation by judicial penalties. Even then there are failures in law enforcement techniques and sometimes courts make mistakes in the finding of guilt. That every guilty person should be punished and every innocent person acquitted is a target which human beings are incapable of reaching.

Moral philosophers have not been slow to recognize these anomalies. Bosanquet asserted that the equivalence of punishment and offence was a meaningless superstition and that society had no means of measuring either the moral guilt of the offender or the pain he suffered on being punished. Hegel admitted that the equation theory had introduced much difficulty into the notion of retribution. The conclusion must be that the concept of retribution does not give the courts specific guidance as to how much punishment to inflict. All it does is to establish that punishment is necessary and that it must look back to an offence which has been committed.

Further criticism of the theory expounded by Kant is directed to the inexorable demand it makes for the infliction of pain or loss on an offender whether any benefit is to be gained from it or not. Does it serve a useful purpose or is it an end in itself? The Bible insists that human beings are precious in the sight of God and many philosophers agree that human beings are ends in themselves and not merely means to other ends. It would appear, therefore, that punishment for its own sake whether or not it brings benefit to the individual or society offends against the dignity of man. It could fairly be described as useless cruelty. When the purpose of punishment is less than an exercise which produces good effects on human beings it must be pronounced both immoral and irrational.[11]

This kind of criticism led to the rise of a new school of thought in the eighteenth century when utilitarian philosophy demanded drastic revision of the penal system on humanitarian lines. Credit for initiating the new thinking on the subject is usually given to Beccaria (1716–1781), Professor of Political Economy in Turin. His principles were grasped by Jeremy Bentham (1748–1832), a British philosopher who led a crusade for the more enlightened use of punishment as a means of social defence. A major principle of utilitarian philosophy was that laws were made for man and their observance is only a means to the promotion of human happiness. Policies were to be judged by whether they produced the maximum of pleasure and the minimum of pain for the majority of the population. The purpose of punishment was not to avenge crime but to prevent it. To punish only because an offence had been committed was simply to add a second evil, unless some useful consequences ensued. Bentham was concerned about making punishment serve human welfare.

The first benefit to society which the utilitarians envisaged was that potential offenders might be deterred when they saw what was done to the lawbreaker who received an exemplary sentence. The severity of the punishment was to be determined by its deterrent effect. Each transgression should be punished by the infliction of as much pain as would suffice to terrify others from doing the same thing. This aim was recognized by the Deuteronomic writer in the Old Testament. Judges were to impose the death penalty for rebellious and disruptive conduct, not merely as an act of vengeance but in order that the people might hear and fear and never again commit such evil (Deut. 17.13; 19.20; 21.22–23).

Although the use of punishment for its practical value seemed more rational than punishment for its own sake, the view that crime could be prevented by an appeal to fear proved to be mistaken. When a certain penalty was imposed and it failed to deter, the severity of the punishment had to be intensified until the required amount of terror was reached in order to prevent crime. It was on the deterrent principle and not the retributive idea that Draco in ancient Greece imposed the death penalty for the theft of a cabbage stalk. The deterrent theory is capable of justifying the most cruel and barbarous penalties. The tempted man must be convinced that crime does not pay. In order to deter potential offenders the punishment must cancel out any gain which the crime has won. The greater the temptation the more severe the penalty.

It was this argument which accounted for the widespread use of capital punishment in the eighteenth century. There were two hundred offences which carried the death penalty. Executions were carried out in public with large crowds assembling to witness the spectacle. Sometimes as many as forty would be hanged in one day. Children were put to death for petty stealing. A lad of fourteen was hanged for the theft of a handkerchief. By such drastic methods it was thought that society would be protected from the law-breaking which was threatening the good order of the nation. The rulers believed that the public, seeing the executions taking place and knowing the consequences of crime, would be induced to keep the law.

When this policy was clearly not having the desired effect, the authorities sought to make the penalty mysterious by shrouding the torture in secrecy. Transportation to the colonies was notoriously cruel. The offender was removed from public gaze and people were left to imagine the suffering it entailed. Small children were thrown into the ships with desperate convicts. A boy of seven was transported for life and one of ten years arrived in Van Dieman's land after having served three years imprisonment. There were many cases of flogging. Details were kept as to when blood was drawn and whether the victim cried or fainted. On some of the vessels the boys were so young they could hardly dress themselves. The mystery which attended the removal of criminals to distant lands was expected to strike terror into the hearts of the tempted.[12]

Such barbarous penalties may seem cruel and unjust to the modern mind, but they have to be seen in the light of the theory on which they were based, namely, that the community could be protected by fear and that to have the desired effect punishment must be brutal. One of the reasons why the theory persisted was that it is impossible to determine how many people are deterred from committing crime by the mode of punishment in operation. It is possible to argue that the volume of crime would have been much larger without such deterrents. Research projects have used statistical methods in order to discover how far the murder rate is affected by capital punishment. In the USA Dr Thorston Sellin studied global statistics and concluded that the incidence of murder bore no relation to the penalties imposed.

Although the utilitarians appealed to humanitarian ideals in supporting the deterrent theory the results of its implementation were far from benevolent. Even the most spectacular and brutal penalties proved unable to prevent crime. It was a mistake to believe that hanging would deter a thief, for the mind of the criminal does not generally consider how to avoid pain. Strong psychological pressures overrule calculations of consequences. Many offenders see themselves as martyrs, and they gain prestige in the eyes of their fellows by reason of the amount of suffering they can bear. The early Christian martyrs went joyfully to their death during the persecutions. In any case offenders expect to avoid detection and conviction, so the nature of the penalty is not germane to their thinking.

Beccaria put forward this criticism: as long as there was a reasonable chance of evading punishment the severity of the penalty was not important to the felon, he said. Crimes were more certainly prevented by the certainty than by the severity of punishment, he added. He also made the valuable point that the ruling authorities should set an example to the community. Their public actions should be capable of being copied by individual citizens. The punishment of death, he maintained, was pernicious to society because of the example of barbarity which it afforded.[13]

Another critic has made the point that exemplary punishments are based on a false premise. They assume that an individual may be sacrificed for the supposed good which might accrue to the nation. The offender is a person of value and may not be used as a pawn for the protection of the realm. As N. L. Robinson has put it:

> To seek anything less than the highest good of even the most erring member of society is not to protect society but to injure it. The rights of society are not really vindicated by denying the deepest right of the individual to be treated as of infinite worth. To hold the individual cheap is to hold society cheap too.[14]

The deterrent theory may have been an advance on the doctrine of retribution in that it expected punishment to have some useful function in society rather than merely defending an abstract principle, but it failed to satisfy the conviction that the good of the individual cannot be sacrificed to the good of the state. It has been used to justify the most savage penalties without achieving the desired end. It failed to take into account the psychology of the criminal, who either does not weigh the consequences of his crime or else hopes to avoid detection and conviction. It sees morality as based on fear and this has the effect of encouraging clandestine rebellion and hypocrisy.

The second suggestion put forward by the utilitarians for deriving social benefit from the penalites inflicted was that the aim of punishment should be the improvement of the character of the offender. The idea that the purpose of punishment should be the reformation of the wrong-doer himself deserves careful study, for if the criminal is turned away from his evil ways the requirements of morality will be met. There can be no better way of protecting society than by curing the offender. If punishment can secure the reformation of the malefactor it might be a useful tool of social control.

It was Bishop Butler who coined the aphorism 'Spare the rod and spoil the child.' He was paraphrasing some of the frequent injunctions of Israel's proverbs, as for example:

He who spares the rod hates his son, but he who loves him is diligent to discipline him (Prov. 13.24).

Jewish fathers had abundant encouragement to resort to corporal punishment in the oft-repeated command to use the rod. Predictions of the moral corruption which would follow in the wake of neglected discipline were frequent. An obedient child would give the father a peaceful life, while an unpunished rascal would bring shame on his mother (Prov. 29.15–17). There is always the danger, however, that the goal may not be the happiness of the person punished but the honour of the parents and the esteem of the neighbours.

What the utilitarians had in mind was that penal suffering added a self-regarding motive for obeying the law. Human beings are normally averse to suffering and shrink from what is disagreeable. When the idea of pain is associated with the committing of crime there would be an incentive to do right. This mechanical interpretation of behaviour motivation was prominent in the eighteenth century. It was believed that outward behaviour could be controlled by fear. It did not seem to matter what happened to the inward disposition. Parents and teachers have learnt that a moral response based on fear was liable to cause emotional disturbance and produce hypocritical profession and secret rebellion.

As far as the treatment of criminals was concerned the new thinking of Bentham and others revolutionized the prison system. The idea caught on that compulsory detention in prison could improve the character of the inmate and make him a better man by the time he came out. John Howard[15] visited jails all over the country and concluded that they were schools of vice rather than moral clinics. He selected three features for special condemnation. The first was the indiscriminate herding of all kinds of offender in conditions which were detrimental to the physical and moral health of the prisoners. He advocated separate cabins or small rooms so that the inmate could have privacy, especially at night.

His second criticism was that the prisoners spent their time in idleness and debauchery, which did nothing to improve their character. He did not recommend compulsory labour, but he thought that those who wanted to work should be given some task which would occupy their minds and break the monotony. Since then prisons have operated schemes of penal labour which produced nothing but sweat, discomfort and frustration, but eventually they introduced useful industries and vocational training designed to enable the detainee to establish himself in the industrial world on release.

Howard's third suggestion was that a chaplain would be an asset to every jail and that religious services, such as he had seen in Rotterdam, should be regularly held in British prisons. The experiment at Millbank (1816–1843) gave full scope for the reformation of criminals by compulsory attendance at religious services,[16] while the new regime based on the Pentonville model from 1842 onwards regarded solitary confinement in a prison cell as the most potent of all reformative agencies.[17] More recently libraries, educational classes, welfare skills, parole and after-care have tried to make prison a place of rehabilitation.

What needs to be acknowledged, however, is that all these helpful and constructive measures, which have followed Howard's dramatic intervention, are not really forms of punishment. The nub of the reformative theory is that the character of the offender is improved, not by the features which mitigate the punitive sentence, but by the pain inflicted by incarceration in an institution and by the deprivation of liberty. Detention in prison is the penalty – has this any reformative value?

There are two points which support an affirmative answer. One is that before the process of reformation can begin the offender must acknowledge his guilt, and the most effective way of producing penitence is to inflict pain or loss upon him. Corporal punishment may be defended as a method of inducing contrition, especially if it follows quickly on the heels of the offence. The other is that an offender may refrain from crime for fear of punishment, and may eventually form habits of good behaviour under compulsion which may be maintained for better reasons. Compulsory conformity can sometimes lead to a voluntary acceptance of a new way of life. A magistrate told John Howard that he had known persons come out of houses of correction thoroughly reformed and grateful for their confinement.

A contrary view is expressed by other writers. Their argument is that punishment may just as easily turn the attention of the wrong-doer away from his guilt and induce self-pity rather than repentance. Some rebels are not mellowed by brutality, and the infliction of pain may inspire defiance and a desire for revenge. In any case conformity based on fear of consequences may prevent the miscreant from reaching a stage of maturity and responsibility. Some unfortunate people are like puppets on a string – they tamely obey the commands of others. Enforced morality in penal institutions tends to produce 'sociopaths' – people who meekly obey orders and are unable to cope with freedom on release.[18]

Prison administrators know how difficult it is to *force* their wards to keep the rules. Jailers can bring a great deal of pressure on belligerent inmates. They can make life unbearable for their rebels, but there is a limit to what can be achieved by coercion. When a prisoner has been goaded into a mood of reckless abandon, he may invite his captors to do their worst, and when they find there is nothing more they can do he becomes a hero and a martyr in the eyes of his fellow rogues. As Gresham Sykes has put it:

> Coercive tactics may check blatant disobedience, but if the great mass of criminals are to be brought into the habit of conformity it must be on other grounds.[19]

The aim of imprisonment is clearly stated in the first prison rule, namely that 'the training and treatment of convicted prisoners shall be to encourage and assist them to live a good and useful life.' This is now being regarded as unrealistic. Officials are now thinking in terms of management and control. Penologists are talking of the collapse of the rehabilitation ideal. Some of them would like to revert to the 'justice model' and impose fixed sentences with no thought of using prison to improve the character. Others want a renewed emphasis on rehabilitation but they say it should be outside the prison system. There is a strong demand for reducing the prison population by making greater use of non-custodial methods. It is becoming more and more obvious that prison has failed by and large to achieve the reformation of the offender.

The reason for this failure is that we have tried to combine several theories of the aim of punishment into one policy, and the administration of justice is shot through with fundamental inconsistencies. This was overtly stated by Dr William Temple when he was Archbishop of York, in 1934. Retribution was to be the first and primary aim – to show society's repudiation of the offence. The second was deterrence – the shame of conviction would serve to fulfil this purpose. The third aim was reformation – which alone conferred upon the other two the full quality of justice.[20] The conflict between these three aims has produced the penal crisis of today. It has become clear that penalties which degrade a person are inimical to his reformation. To quote Hermann Mannheim:

> Penal reform has to face the undeniable fact that its whole field is permeated with fundamental inconsistencies, a fact which makes it so difficult to pursue a consistent policy.[21]

Mannheim dealt at some length with the principle of 'less eligibility' or 'non-superiority'. The argument is that the condition of the offender should not be more comfortable than those of the poorest member of the non-criminal population. Punishment would lose its deterrent value, as Bentham had pointed out, if offenders were given special privileges of training and treatment which were denied to the innocent. Any attempt to cure the criminal by giving him privileges is frowned upon by the public, and this dilemma has hindered penal reform. This is illustrated in the old jibe, 'If you are unemployed, pinch a lady's handbag and the probation officer will find you a job.'[22]

That the offender often needs positive discrimination to compensate for the deprivation which has led him into crime is one of the considerations which have inspired a radical view of punishment akin to the revolutionary teaching of Jesus and Paul. Progressive thinkers are saying that the whole system of criminal justice has been tried and found wanting. The writing is on the wall. George Bernard Shaw summed up the position of the radicals like this:

> If you are to punish a man retributively you must injure him. If you are to reform him you must improve him. And men are not improved by injuries.[23]

At the present time society is facing a crisis similar to that which faced Beccaria, Bentham and Howard. The radical view cries out for consideration. Punishment is said to be a mistake and a sin. Such a view will seem outrageous to respectable citizens and its advocates will doubtless be condemned as irresponsible visionaries.

One of these visionaries was Margaret Wilson. She surveyed the various methods of punishment used over the centuries and in her book *The Crime of Punishment* published in 1931 she concluded:

> Considering the history of our cruelty, it seems that what we need more than anything else is to cleanse our minds from the idea of judicially exacting suffering for wrong doing, and to realise that our habit of punishment is as great an evil as any crime.[24]

In 1969 Karl Menninger, an American psychiatrist, used the same title for a book in which he says the attempt to combine incompatible philosophies of punishment and reformation still divides penologists and confuses the public. He concludes:

> We must renounce the philosophy of punishment, the obsolete, vengeful penal attitude. In its place we should seek a comprehensive, constructive social attitude – therapeutic in some instances, restraining in others, but preventive in its total social impact.[25]

Such radical views would have seemed crazy at one time. Voices cried in the wilderness but were often reduced to whispers. Now they are being taken seriously. This century has seen the introduction of a number of humanitarian measures which correspond to the strenuous teaching of Jesus Christ and the theology of the cross. These include the probation system, a programme of remedial education for juveniles in community homes, training provisions in Youth Custody establishments, a psychiatric prison at Grendon Underwood, the abolition of capital punishment and flogging of prisoners, the open prison, pre-release hostels, a state system of after-care of discharged prisoners and the alternatives to prison such as community service orders and Attendance Centres.

Add to these amazing achievements the challenge which comes from progressive movements in overseas countries. In Holland, for example, the prison population has been drastically reduced and the probation system is no longer under the courts but is directly related to the client. It is claimed that in spite of these reforms the Dutch have had no greater increase in crime rates than have other countries. When experiments yield good results in one nation there is encouragement to others to imitate them.[26]

In our search for the guidance of the spirit of truth in post-biblical history we have seen how the various aims of punishment revealed in the Bible have been discussed and applied, and the trend has been towards an approval of the radical teaching of the gospel. Humility and mercy, which seem so dangerous to traditionalists, are seen by many penologists to have immense social value. The facts of experience are convincing an increasing number of citizens that society is most surely protected when the criminal turns from his evil ways and co-operates with his fellow-men. This is not only a plea for evangelism in prisons in order to seek a conversion experience through religious faith; it is also an appeal to Christians to initiate and support programmes of education and propaganda for the achievement of a more positive and constructive response to the problem of crime.

Christianity recognizes the sinfulness of man and does not expect too much, but Christian hope enables it not to expect too little.

9 THE RELEVANCE OF AN IDEAL

The Christian who is committed to the radical ethic of Jesus finds himself in a dilemma when his involvement in an imperfect world demands compromise. His earthly citizenship involves participation in the judicial system of the secular state. His personal morality tells him to forgive those who wrong him, but it gives him no mandate to impose his ideals upon the community whose rulers are committed to the protection of their subjects from the attacks of criminals. Although he belongs to a 'kingdom not of this world', he is also a member of a nation state and is expected to participate in the framing and enforcing of the laws of his country.

Faced with such bifurcation he finds that his life is characterized by tension. He is 'in the world but not of it.' He has to render to Caesar the things that are Caesar's and to God the things that are God's. There is a contradiction between social responsibility and his ethical ideal. The Bible recognizes this tension and offers no escape from it. We have to explore the relevance of the ideal to the real and study the strategy of Christian witness in the context of inevitable compromise.

According to the gospels Jesus saw the role of a disciple as influencing the social policies of the secular state so that its organization might approximate more and more to the Christian ideal. He said his followers were to be 'the light of the world', like seed growing secretly or like leaven in the meal (Matt. 5.13–14; Mark 4.26–7; Matt. 13.33). They were to offer the grace of God by which peoples' life-style might be changed. They were invited to practise the ethic of love, even in a hostile environment. But they had no mandate to opt out of the life of the community even if sub-Christian standards were guiding their neighbours. Jesus said, 'I do not pray that thou shouldst take them out of the world, but that thou shouldst keep them from the evil one' (John 17.15).

In order that the modern Christian may understand the effect of this tension between state and church he could do worse than examine some of the attitudes of ecclesiastical leaders during the Christian era. What has been the strategy of the church in its relationship with the state? How have our ancestors applied Bible teaching to the subject of penal reform? The answer would seem to be that they have been as confused and inconsistent as those who produced holy writ. Nevertheless some useful lessons can be learned from their efforts to deal with tension.

The early centuries of the period saw a serious attempt on the part of the followers of Jesus to contract out of the social order and so to avoid involvements in the penal policies of the state. Jesus had been crucified by the representative of the Roman emperor in Judaea, and some of the later emperors were intent on destroying his religious movement. Hundreds of Christians were executed for disobedience to imperial edicts. When it was a criminal offence merely to profess Christianity, there seemed to be no alternative to contracting out of a hostile regime. How could a minority group be expected to subscribe to the enforcement of laws which were designed to destroy it?

When the climate became more favourable and Christians were allowed political status, the question to be faced was: Is it permissible for church members to sit as magistrates in the criminal courts? Some accepted the office, others refused. The uncertainty may have been due to the varying attitudes of Roman authorities to the church, or there may have been a wavering concerning the relevance of the radical ethic of Jesus. In any case, by the third century it was definitely decided that Christian baptism should be refused to any who had become magistrates except on condition that they quit their office. The reason given was that the judging of one's fellow-men and the infliction of physical injury on an offender were incompatible with the Christian ethic.

Tertullian explained that certain acts performed by magistrates were inadmissible in a true servant of Christ. He declared:

As to the duties of civil power the Christian must not decide on anyone's life or honour – about money it is permissible; but he must bind no one, nor imprison and torture any.

According to this notable exponent of Christian discipline to sentence even a slave to death, to imprison the debtor, or to put the household of a suspected criminal to the rack, though the duty of a magistrate, would for a Christian be a sin.[1]

With the conversion to Christianity of the emperor Constantine in 312, the possibility of partnership between church and state began to be seen. This seemed like a triumph for the case of Christ. Constantine not only legalized Christian worship, but he initiated a policy of penal reform. He forbade the infliction of capital punishment, except when the accused confessed his crime or when the testimony of witnesses was unanimous. He laid down that criminals were no longer to be branded on the face, that debtors were not to be scourged and that prisoners must not be kept in dark dungeons or unnecessarily loaded with chains.[2]

In the light of these reforms it seemed to many Christians that they could now co-operate in the administration of justice in the imperial courts, though there were some who felt such co-operation to be unacceptable to their conscience. The price they had to pay was the stifling of the Christian witness to what they saw as a more excellent way of dealing with criminals. They were convinced that their stance had been justified when a later emperor, Julian, systematically removed from office all Christians whose conscience forbade them to carry out executions.

The partnership between church and state was again challenged by the attempt of Christians to shield criminals from the rigours of judicial punishment. From the fifth century onwards the place of worship became a refuge for the fugitive from justice. The Israelite cities of refuge had created a precedent for this device. At first only minor offenders were given shelter, but in 511 the Council of Orléans laid down that no criminal who sought refuge in a church or a bishop's house should be dragged from it, and this was re-enacted by Pope Boniface V (619–25). With minor alterations the law of sanctuary persisted for hundreds of years. The church was resisting the penal methods of the state.

There was, of course, a limit to the number of fugitives for whom the church could offer protection and care. At first the offender was expected to surrender to the civil authorities after forty days, when, if he promised to quit the realm, he would be allowed to travel in safety to the nearest port. When large numbers elected to emigrate in order to avoid punishment, the period allowed for surrender was extended, with the result that whole colonies of fugitives from justice were finding permanent shelter in the great abbeys of Britain.

This was not a satisfactory system. The church was unable to exercise adequate supervision over the malefactors under its roof, especially as many of them were venturing out to commit further crimes. In such cases the Pope gave permission for their removal from sanctuary. It was also conceded that a number of serious offences should be excluded from privilege. As the power of the state increased further restrictions were imposed on the sanctuaries and, with the dissolution of the monasteries, the system virtually came to an end. In 1604 the laws about sanctuaries were repealed and in 1623 all rights of refuge were taken away.[3]

That there was a commitment to the ethic of Jesus which caused the early church to contract out of the secular system of criminal justice is illustrated by a passage in the second century apology known as the Epistle of Diognetus:

> Was he (Jesus) sent think you as a man might suppose to establish sovereignty, to inspire fear and terror? Not so, but in gentleness and meekness has he sent him, as a king might send a son who is a king. He sent him as sending God; he sent him as a man unto men; He sent him as a saviour, as using persuasion and not force; for force is no attribute of God. He sent him as entreating, not as persecuting; he sent him as loving, not as judging.[4]

Another interesting attempt to ease the tension between those who accepted the radical ethic of Jesus and those who administered the state's judicial system was the emergence of the dual system in which the church accepted responsibility for dealing with its own recalcitrant members and allowed the state full scope to deal with the rest of the population. Had not Paul enjoined the Corinthians not to take their own grievances to the secular courts, but to deal with them according to their own standards within the fellowship of the church? Recognizing the dilemma of the Christians, Constantine allowed them to set up their own courts, parallel with the imperial tribunals, for the correction of their erring members. It was judicial apartheid.

At first the ecclesiastical courts restricted the privilege to clergy, but eventually anyone connected with the church claimed the right to plead 'clergy' and be tried by his fellow-believers. On the whole the penalties imposed by the church were lenient. Capital punishment and mutilation were no part of the armoury of ecclesiastical authorities. Most of their penalties were along the lines of penitential discipline, such as fasting and pilgrimage, designed for the cure of the soul. Their most powerful weapon was excommunication, which meant that the offender could be handed over to the secular magistrate.

Penitential fasts were a common form of punishment in church courts. An offender could be ordered to live on bread and water for so many days or even years for serious crimes. Abbots had no qualms about using corporal punishment. Floggings were frequently administered. The younger monks would normally receive thirty-nine stripes. The church was so powerful in the middle ages that it could bring kings to their knees. Henry II is reported to have been severely scourged by a group of bishops who each gave him five strokes until he became ill.[5]

The severity of monastic discipline in the middle ages raises doubt as to whether the vision of a more excellent way of dealing with offenders had faded. The idea of the church dealing with its own members in a superior way brought little credit to the abbots. An example is the case of an erring brother named John, who, in 1283, was accused of biting his prior's finger. The bishop ordered the offender to be kept in prison under iron chains and on a strict diet until he was penitent. Another recalcitrant monk was given a severe flogging and consigned to be fettered in a cell. He died and was buried with the chains still on the corpse.[6]

Although the monasteries were places where the religious could withdraw from the world and leave the earthly kingdom to its own devices, the punishments which prevailed were hardly less severe than those they had left behind. One of these was solitary confinement. Some of the monks subjected to it died in all the agonies of despair. King John was asked to intervene and he issued an ordinance that the superior should visit and console the prisoners and should allow other monks to visit them twice a month. Solitude was defended on the grounds that it was therapeutic. The irony of the situation was that secular authorities had to step in and interfere in the name of humanity.

In the twelfth century there were a number of cases of murder and rape committed by clerics. They were committed to prison by the bishops. The king demanded that one of them be hanged. Not only had this rogue committed murder, but he had also abused the judge. The bishop tried to appease the king. He had the offender stripped and flogged in the presence of the angry judge and then banished for two years, but the king still thought the offending cleric should have gone to the gallows. Such incidents led eventually to the abolition of the dual system and so it came to pass that all accused persons should be tried in the secular courts when common law was infringed.

The movement to give the state power to over-rule the church has come to be known as Erastianism. Erastus is the Greek name of a professor at Heidelberg and later at Basel, Thomas Lieber (1521–1584), who argued for the complete subordination of the ecclesiastical to the secular power. He had a high estimate of the church's spiritual character and could not tolerate its use of coercion in the interest of religion. He denied that the church had the right to inflict excommunication, because such a penalty entailed secular hardships and should only be prescribed by the state. He wanted the power of the church to be restricted. He held that the religious organization should not dictate how the state should exercise its function. Those who defended the right of the church to tell the state what to do were called Ultramontanists. That these two schools existed is an illustration of the tension between the two institutions.

There were two kinds of offence against which the Christian church showed no mercy. One was heresy. The brutality which characterized the Inquisition was far from the ethic of non-resistance to evil proclaimed by the sermon on the mount. In 1478 Torquemada, prior of the Dominican convent at Sergovia, was appointed Grand Inquisitor, and in the course of two years more than two thousand heretics are said to have been burned alive. The tribunal for the examination and punishment of heretics operated in Spain from the thirteenth century, was introduced to parts of France and Italy but never operated as such in England. According to the historian Llorente, the number of victims of the Spanish inquisition from 1481 to 1808 was 341,521, of whom 32,000 were burned.[7]

The other offence against which the church's record was blemished was witchcraft. According to Lecky tens of thousands of victims perished by the most agonizing and protracted torments without exciting the faintest compassion. People with abnormal physical structure, such as having three teats instead of two, people who lived alone or kept a black cat were suspected of being witches. Witchcraft was made a felony in England in 1541 and the last legal witch trial was in 1712. It has been estimated that during the sixteenth and seventeenth centuries the witch death roll in Europe reached 200,000 people, Britain's share being 30,000.

Now these witch hunts were carried out by secular authorities, but they were condoned and even supported by the church. Tension was eased when both institutions agreed on a campaign. Theology and law joined hands. In the middle of the seventeenth century, Matthew Hopkins of Manningtree became a professional witch 'discoverer' and his campaign was based on the Bible, where he found the command, 'You shall not permit a sorceress to live' (Ex. 22.18). Disbelief in witchcraft was tantamount to disbelief in Christianity. To give up belief in witches meant giving up the Bible.[8] Tension was reduced when the radical ethic of love gave way to a crusade of hate.

The reformation brought a new insight into the problem of church and state. Luther proclaimed the doctrine of the two kingdoms – sacred and secular, spiritual and worldly, religious and political, law and gospel. There would always be tension between them. The radical ethic of Jesus was applicable to the first but not the second. The earthly kingdom needed laws and the power to punish individuals who threatened its security. Because of sin the world was suffering from the 'fall' and was incapable of reaching the standard set by the gospel. We should not expect to see mercy operating in the secular courts and we should not witness vengeance in the church. So Luther was accused of supporting dual standards and of allowing a large measure of autonomous rule to the state. He has even been regarded as politically passive.

It is probably a mistake to say that Luther washed his hands of the secular government. For him both church and state were grounded in the divine decree. But while God offers mercy in the gospel his wrath is made manifest in the state. It is quite impossible to renounce power in a fallen world, he said. Coercion was necessary but it is integrated into a paternal relationship of love. In order to defend the weak against injustice God provided the protection of force, but love was the motive which validated the rule of power.

It is not easy to see wrath and severity as aspects of love in some of Luther's utterances. For example:

A prince and lord must remember that he is God's minister and servant of his wrath, to whom the sword is committed, and he sins against God if he does not fulfil the duties of his office. . . . If he can punish and does not, even though the punishment consists in the taking of life and the shedding of blood, then he is guilty of all the murders and all the evil which these fellows commit. Here there is no place for patience and mercy. It is the time for the sword, not the day of grace.[9]

Exponents of Luther's doctrine have underlined his defence of the criminal justice system of the secular state. Philip Watson emphasized that God's justice is an expression of his love.

Justice is a subordinate instrument of love in an evil world. The penalties should be adapted to reform as well as punish the criminal. The whole system of the State ought to be framed to serve the purposes of love.[10]

Recalling the words of Jesus about Christians being the 'salt of the earth', Watson says the church is the conscience of the state and should provide an antidote to the diseases of society.

Lutheran dualism does not provide a licence for the secular courts to do what they like. Reformation theology rules out oppression of minority groups in a totalitarian regime. Paul's defence of civil magistrates does not imply that the church has to contract out of the penal policies of the nation. If love is the motive which validates the rule of power, then the church has the right to be involved in politics as a watchdog and to pass judgment on the judges. In other words the state need not be afraid of Erastianism as long as Christian groups are allowed to suggest and persuade, rather than coerce and control, the government in power. Members of the Reformed churches are ready to render to Caesar the things that are Caesar's as long as they are not precluded from rendering to God the things that are God's.

For John Calvin, however, there was no room for tension as there was no distinction between church and state. The law was the form of the gospel and the gospel was the content of the law. Whereas Luther saw the Old Testament as the background against which the light of the gospel shone forth, his fellow-reformer saw the Old Testament as a light in its own right. The Law of Moses was not superseded but fulfilled. Israel's rulers had received their commission from God, and contemporary rulers had legal directives in the same way. This is the significance of legalism in Calvinism. Christ had embraced some of the features of law and was the head of both church and world.

It followed that for Calvin every government had to be a Christian government. The political order was not alien. The two kingdoms did not stand over against one another. The earthly kingdom had to be a reflection of the heavenly kingdom. God was sovereign lord over all nations. The church had the duty to direct the affairs of state and tell the statesmen what to do. They demanded that the civil powers punish any contempt of God and any malicious offence against his word. Blasphemy had to be forcibly repudiated. The aim of the church was the perfecting of life on the earth.

This was the theology behind the Puritan movement in the sixteenth and seventeenth centuries when the religious bodies invoked the arm of the secular penal system for the enforcement of Christian morality. If the Catholic church had been strong enough to control national policies and bring monarchs to their knees, why should Calvinism not do the same? When ecclesiastical authorities believed there was a divine command that citizens should attend divine worship on Sunday, the coercive power of the state was deployed to enforce such attendance. In Sheffield, for example, in 1790, nine men were locked in the stocks for drinking in a public house when they should have been in church. In Edinburgh in 1560 it was enacted that all persons found guilty of blasphemy should be ordered to wear the brank, an iron bridle with a sharp spike fitting into the mouth.

Christian standards of sexual conduct were enforced with the strong arm of the law. At the quarter sessions in Devon in 1598 it was decided that mothers of illegitimate children were to be whipped. A little while later a ducking-stool was brought into operation in Hull for the punishment of fornicators. In 1563 the Scottish parliament made adultery a capital offence, while in America in 1662 three persons were executed for that breach of the Christian moral code.[11]

Calvin's attempt to overcome the tension between church and state by bringing the secular powers under a Christian law based on the Old Testament foundered on the rocks of a defective christology. It assumed that the radical ethic of Jesus was not applicable to secular rulers. If the church could accept the divine right of kings and support capital punishment, as in the Westminster Confession and in article XXXVII of the Church of England, there was little room for tension between religious and secular authorities.

In his detailed discussion of the church and politics Thielicke admits that the Bible gives no direct guidance as to how secular authorities should deal with transgressors of the law, but it does provide clarification on ethical issues to assist individual Christians in the exercise of conscience. The church has to address in a responsible way the people to whom the orders of this aeon are entrusted by virtue of their political office.[12]

A similar point has been made by Sir Norman Anderson who argued that, while the Christian should support law-enforcement by the state, obedience to the secular government is not absolute. A nation may not demand support when it fails to promote virtue and uphold natural justice.[13]

As an institution the Christian church has not been too eager to make detailed judgments on penal affairs, but historical records show that there has been abundant scope for individual believers to take an active part in campaigns to humanize justice. Members of various Christian communions have personally advocated policies to bring the administration of the criminal courts into harmony with the ethical ideal of Jesus.

John Howard (1726–90) was an independent by religion. When he was appointed High Sheriff of the county of Bedford he began to investigate the conditions in the county jails of England and Wales. His findings were published in 1777, and led to significant changes in the administration of prisons. He alleged that the indiscriminate herding of criminals in common dungeons was not only physically unhealthy but also detrimental to morals. Jails had become schools of crime, he said. He was called to the bar of the House of Commons to make suggestions for prison reform and his aim was to make imprisonment a therapeutic experience. His deep concern for the welfare of offenders was inspired by his religious faith.

John Wesley considered Howard to be one of the greatest men in Europe. He wrote:

> Mr. Howard is really an extraordinary man; God has raised him up to be a blessing to many nations. Nothing but the mighty power of God can enable him to go through his difficult and dangerous employments.[14]

Howard was inspired by Wesley. After their first meeting he said:

> I was encouraged to go on vigorously with my designs. I saw in him how much a single man may achieve by zeal and perseverance and I thought: 'Why may I not do as much in my way as Mr. Wesley has done in his, if only I am as persevering and assiduous?', and I

determined I would pursue my work with more alacrity than ever.[15]

John Wesley visited prisoners in Oxford Castle and in Newgate prison, and his followers, notably Sarah Peters and Silas Told, regularly offered divine grace to condemned criminals at the gallows. The Methodists proclaimed that 'the vilest offender may turn and find grace.' They were not noted for advocating penal reform but their emphasis on the mercy of God helped to create a new climate in which the savage punishments of the eighteenth century could be challenged.

Of the many Church of England pioneers in the field of penal reform the name of Sir Samuel Romilly should be underlined. In 1810 he launched a campaign to reduce the number of capital offences in Britain. He proposed that the offence of stealing up to five shillings worth of goods from a shop should no longer carry the death penalty. As a barrister he resolved that the business of his life would be to render service to his country and his fellow-citizens. Influenced by Howard and Beccaria he became a member of parliament and carried out his resolve in the sphere of penal reform.

His main argument was that official barbarity produced cruelty in people who observed it. He told parliament:

> I call upon you to remember that cruel punishments have an inevitable tendency to produce cruelty in people. It is not by destruction of tenderness – it is not by exciting revenge, that we can hope to generate virtuous conduct in those confined to our care. You may cut out the heart of a sufferer and hold it up to the view of the populace, and you may imagine that you serve the community; but the real effect of such scenes is to torture the compassionate and to harden the obdurate. You will not diminish offences by teaching the subjects to look with indifference upon human suffering. Fury will retaliate the cruelties which it has been accustomed to behold.[16]

There were those who accused Romilly of being retained for the Dissenters, but he denied that he had ever entered a Nonconformist meeting house, even out of curiosity. He assured his critics that he had always attended services of the established church in which he had been educated. In private devotions he sought divine aid to improve his faculties and quicken his ardour for the public good. He hoped he might prove a humble instrument in the divine work of enlarging the sphere of human happiness.

The confusion associated with the Christian ethic's incursion into politics is vividly seen in the results of Romilly's reform bills. Here is an individual with the highest of religious motives proposing that minor shop-lifting should no longer be a capital offence, yet his efforts were frustrated by official prelates of the Church of England to which he himself belonged. When the bill came to the House of Lords, the Lord Chancellor, Lord Ellenborough, defended the existing law on the grounds that the social order depended upon it and that if it were altered they would not know whether they were on their heads or their feet. He was supported by the Archbishop of Canterbury and six bishops. Crushed and defeated, Romilly took his own life. The campaign went on, however, and the historians say that as punishments became less severe crime decreased.[17]

Even as late as 1948, when the abolition of the death penalty was being discussed in the House of Lords, Dr Haigh, Bishop of Winchester, defended the status quo. He said 'We must be satisfied by the strongest reasons that we are not interfering *arbitrarily* and *needlessly* with so *happy* a balance of forces as are embodied in our administration of the death penalty at this time' (Hansard). It can surely never be untimely to consider a punishment like hanging.

Moberly expressed surprise that officials of the Christian community have been so complacent in supporting penal reform:

> On the face of it, the influence of Christianity might have been expected to make for abolition of punishment, or at least for its great alleviation. . . . It is suggested in many quarters that the Church has failed in its moral teaching because it has not been prepared to take some of the most arresting and revolutionary elements in the Gospel at their face value.[18]

One of John Howard's proposals was that every prison should have a chaplain and he wistfully hoped that the clergyman chosen for the post should be a 'Christian'. The experiment at Millbank penitentiary (1816–1843) seemed to provide an opportunity for the church to enter into a real partnership with secular authority. The chaplain was given enormous scope for the exercise of his evangelistic and pastoral office. Previously ministers of religion had complained that conditions in the jails had made their task impossible. Now the priest would have full support in the fulfilment of his mission. The chapel was at the heart of the institution and the Bishop of London's nominee, the Reverend Samuel Bennett, was given the full support of a philanthropic committee.

Special rules were drawn up for the venture. No prisoner was to absent himself from divine worship or behave in an irreverent manner in the chapel. Members of the public were invited to witness the effect of religious exercises on the inmates. It seemed that the problem of reforming offenders was solved. On the other hand there was the difficult task of controlling the captive audience. There were riots in the place of worship and a plot to murder the chaplain.

The next chaplain was the Reverend Daniel Nihil and it was during his term of office that the experiment reached its climax. Nihil was made governor and was in full command of the establishment. Prison officers were to control their temper and give no offence to the inmates. Some of the warders carried bibles under their arms and quoted scripture to their wards. The gospel was on trial. Under the chaplain-governor the church was the dominant partner. The outcome was disappointing. The lesson which emerged was that you cannot force a prisoner to open his heart to God. Not all the coercion of the penitentiary could make a criminal religious. By 1843 Millbank had become an ordinary prison, organized on military lines.[19]

Of all the Christian groups the Society of Friends has probably been the most radical in the area of penal reform. Its founder, George Fox, in the seventeenth century, had himself been incarcerated in various jails around the country for such offences as speaking at meetings without permission and defying various conventions, and he used his experiences to help other prisoners. William Penn had been a prisoner at Newgate before emigrating to America. Elizabeth Fry began her visits to Newgate Prison in 1813. 'I am distressed for your children,' she told the mothers. 'Is there not something we can do for these innocent little ones? I am a mother myself.' As she lifted a filthy child to her bosom she said she had recently given birth to her tenth child. Her technique was to read the Bible to the prisoners. She visited prisons all over the British Isles and was instrumental in arousing interest in what had previously been a closed book.

In America the Quakers opposed the death penalty and with the formation of the Philadelphia Society for Alleviating the Miseries of Public Prisons a new emphasis was laid on penal reform. Unfortunately the introduction of solitary confinement as a reformative discipline, though well intentioned, did not produce the desired results. The Society of Friends has continued to submit memoranda to the government on penal reform and has joined with other churches in a programme of public education on criminal justice.

Various ecumenical groups have been set up by the churches in recent years. The Roman Catholic Church has made a significant contribution. The Division of Social Responsibility of the British Council of Churches has made frequent representations to the Home Office on penal affairs, and the World Council of Churches has convened conferences in order that countries can learn from one another and be enabled to give a more precise definition on how the Christian ethic can be translated into penal policy.

In 1964 the Free Church Council circulated a document around the Nonconformist churches entitled 'Penal Reform'. One paragraph reads:

> It is our conviction that the paramount objective of the penal system should be the rehabilitation of the offender, both in his own interest and for the safety of the public. In the light of modern knowledge of the factors which predispose to delinquency we believe that this objective can only be achieved by positive measures of treatment designed to counteract the pressures which make for crime. Harsh measures of punishment which are designed to humiliate and degrade the offender have no place in a programme which aims at the improvement of his character. The emphasis should be on treatment rather than punishment.[20]

It is essential that when the churches make representation to governments on political issues they have done their homework and that they speak with knowledge of practical difficulties facing those who have to implement them. Working parties on penal reform should include practitioners who have inside knowledge of the judicial system, and the views of academic criminologists have to be sought. The loftiest ideals may come to grief on the rocks of the stern realities of human frailty. In a democratic society the public have to be persuaded before legislation is feasible. The use of the media in creating a favourable climate for reform is part of the church's strategy. Many lessons were learned, for example, during the crusade for the abolition of the death penalty.

Another aspect of the partnership between church and state is the acceptance on the part of Christian citizens of involvement in political and social activities as a vocation, with the intent of influencing professions and institutions towards more enlightened penal policies. Committed Christians do in fact infiltrate secular life as members of parliament, judges and magistrates, prison and probation officers, teachers and social workers. Such involvement makes more sense than contracting out of the secular world on the excuse that one's hands may get soiled or that the world is doomed to pass away.

The New Testament ethic of love may seem to be incapable of realization in this world. However desirable it may be to forgive the wrong-doer, such a policy can only be operated when people have the right disposition. There is a place for pessimism, such as was expressed by Reinhold Niebuhr:

> Men living in nature and in the body, will never be capable of the sublimation of egoism and the attainment of the self sacrifice passion and the complete disinterestedness which the ethic of Jesus demands. . . . It is therefore impossible to construct a socio-moral policy from this religio-moral insight of Jesus, as, for instance, Tolstoi attempted in his objection to jails and other forms of social punishment. The ideals of the best criminologists are still in the realm of unrealised hopes and they will never be fully realised. The ideal in its perfect form lies beyond the capabilities of human nature. . . . A profound religion will not give itself to the illusion that perfect justice can be achieved in a sinful world.[21]

Even if the state can never be perfectly Christian, as Jesus bade his disciples to be, there is no reason why it should not strive to approximate to the ideal. The ultimate penal reform must be the abolition of punishment. This is supported by the radical school of penology, which argues that there is no point in reforming a system which needs to be abolished.

If a humanitarian movement can visualize the day when therapy will replace the system of punishment and decriminalization bring a new sense of responsibility in freedom to the citizen, there is every reason why the Christian should embrace a like ideal. But it will need to be based on the theology of the cross. Moreover militant optimism is an important part of the theology of hope and is a vital element in the biblical doctrine of the Holy Spirit, who sheds abroad in the human heart the love which takes no account of evil and never despairs (I Cor. 13.4–7).

Notes

Introduction

1. H. L. Mansell, *The Limits of Thought*, 1858.
2. J. W. Rogerson, 'The Old Testament and Social and Moral Questions', *The Modern Churchman*, XXV.1, 1982, pp. 28–35.
3. Henry McKeating, *Studying the Old Testament*, Epworth Press 1979, pp. 18–23.

1 Punishment as Vengeance

1. G. E. Mendenhall, 'Covenant Forms in Israelite Tradition', *The Biblical Archaeologist* XVII, 1954, pp. 50–76.
2. A. Phillips, *Ancient Israel's Criminal Law*, Basil Blackwell 1970, ch. 1, but see also D. J. McCarthy, *Old Testament Covenant*, Basil Blackwell 1972.
3. 'The Decalogue was the charter of freedom which Yahweh had presented to the people delivered from Egypt. The people received it, not as a burden, but as a gift, which was seen as a privilege and as an occasion for thanks.' J. J. Stamm with M. E. Andrew in *The Ten Commandments in Recent Research*, SCM Press 1967.
4. Henry McKeating, 'Sanctions against Adultery in Israelite Society', *Journal for the Study of the Old Testament*, 1979, p. 58.
5. George Ives, *A History of Penal Methods*, Stanley Paul, 1914, p. 2.
6. Henry Maine, *Ancient Law*, Dent 1861, p. 389.
7. Robert R. Marett, *Anthropology*, Williams and Norgate 1912, Ch. 7.
8. Dummelow, *Commentary on the Bible*, Macmillan 1909, pp. xxxv–vi.
9. Leslie Davison, *Principles of Penal Reform*, Epworth Press 1960, p. 65.
10. Paul Joyce, 'The Individual and the Community', *Beginning Old Testament Study*, ed. John Rogerson, SPCK 1983, ch. 5.
11. Leo Page, *Crime and the Community*, Faber and Faber 1937.
12. 'In the law code the individual wrongdoer is consistently made responsible in his own person. This is so throughout the Semitic world.' J. R. Porter, 'The Legal Aspects of the Concept of Corporate Personality in the Old Testament', *Vetus Testamentum*, 1965, p. 361.
13. H. Thielicke, *Theological Ethics*, A. & C. Black 1966, vol. I, p. 586.
14. A. A. Van Ruler, quoted in ibid. p. 109.

2 The Concept of Justice

1. The concept of justice was not new. All human societies have some such notion in their legal systems, but it was given a fresh emphasis under the monarchy. The argument for the enthronement of a king was that it would facilitate a just society.
2. 'To the modern mind the Levite, who throws his wife out into the dark street is as guilty as the rabble to whom he surrenders her. But that was not the ancient point of view. This is the story, not of the avenging of a woman's violated honour, but of the vindication of a man's sacred rights of property (in his wife) and the laws of hospitality', James Straham, *Commentary on the Bible*, A. S. Peake, Jack edition 1919, p. 270.

3. Keith W. Whitelam, *The Just King*, JSOT Press 1979, ch. 1.

4. David reigned over the House of Judah in Hebron for over seven years before being annointed king over all Israel (II Sam. 2.11, 5.3–5).

5. In the killing of Abner by Joab blood feud led to an injustice, but common usage left the king powerless to interfere. David followed the bier in order to demonstrate to the public that he was innocent.

6. This anomaly is overcome by saying the Amalekite was lying. See P. Kyle McCarter, *Commentary on II Samuel*, Anchor Bible, Doubleday 1984, p. 64.

7. The king was supposed to uphold the cause of the powerless and prevent such abuses, but he does not interfere. The tension between what the king is expected to do and what he actually does begins to emerge. The significant point is that David is responsible to a higher authority. McCarter, op. cit. pp. 304–7.

8. Rogerson, *Beginning OT Study*, op. cit. ch. 3.

9. A. Phillips, *Ancient Israel's Criminal Law*, Basil Blackwell 1970, ch. 7.

10. Peake's *Commentary*, p. 241.

11. Ives, *History of Penal Methods*, op. cit., p. 8.

12. E.g. Judges 16.21. Grinding at the mill imposed on Samson by the Philistines.

13. Trevor Ling, *A History of Religion East and West*, Macmillan 1968, pp. 74–5.

3   Punishment and Reconciliation

1. Rogerson, *Beginning OT Study*, p. 151.

2. A system which required a member of the family to exact vengeance could not cope with homicide within the family. That it provided a break in the cycle of revenge is important.

3. McKeating, *Studying the OT*, p. 23. A. M. Beck, *A Short History of Israel*, Hodder and Stoughton 1963, p. 34.

4. D. R. Jones, 'Exposition of Isaiah chapter one verses one to nine', *Scottish Journal of Theology* 21, 1968, pp. 320–9.

5. Paul Joyce, in Rogerson, op. cit., ch. 5.

6. Whether this story is history or myth it provides a glimpse of the lengths to which imperial rulers might go in order to enforce the law.

7. The number of offences which can properly be called crimes, actions which the state forbids and seeks to stamp out, is very limited in near-eastern law, though it is considerably augmented in the Old Testament by the large number of religious crimes. See G. J. Wenham, *Book of Leviticus*, Eerdmans 1979, p. 284.

8. The nearest thing to imprisonment in ancient Israel was the restriction imposed on a manslayer, who was bound to live in a city of refuge until the death of the high priest. See Wenham, op. cit., p. 286.

9. Elizabeth Moberly, *Suffering: Innocent and Guilty*, SPCK 1978, chs. 1 and 3.

10. Ibid.

11. C. R. North, *The Suffering Servant in Deutero-Isaiah*, Oxford University Press 1948, pp. 202–7.

12. R. C. Zaehner, *Concise Encyclopaedia of Living Faiths*, Hutchinson 1959, pp. 200–14.

13. O. Kaiser regards this verse as an assurance of a resurrection of the righteous after death and would place its origin in the Hellenistic age. Other scholars, however, see it as an assurance of the rebirth of the Jewish community as in the account of the coming together of the dry bones in Ezekiel 31. See R. E. Clements, *Commentary on Isaiah 1–39*, Marshall, Morgan and Scott 1980, pp. 216–17.

14. Stanley B. Frost, *Old Testament Apocalyptic*, Epworth Press 1952, p. 170.

15. Zaehner, op. cit., p. 208.

4   The Radical Ethic of Jesus

1. W. Moberly, *The Ethics of Punishment*, Faber and Faber 1968, p. 330.

2. N. H. G. Robinson, *The Groundwork of Christian Ethics*, Collins 1971, pp. 25–6.

3. Ibid., pp. 114–15.

4. C. H. Dodd, *Gospel and Law*, Cambridge University Press 1950, pp. 62, 76.

5. T. W. Manson, *Ethics and the Gospel*, SCM Press 1960, p. 48.

6. Ibid., p. 50.

7. Ibid., pp. 170, 280.

8. John Calvin, *Institutes of the Christian Religion*, Bk 3, ch. 7, p. 6.

9. Paul Ramsey, *Basic Christian Ethics*, SCM Press 1950, ch. 5.

10. The people whom the Pharisees wrote off as 'sinners' and whom Jesus accepted were not necessarily criminals, their offences may have been ceremonial. He did, however, form a relationship with despised tax-gatherers and with the thief who was crucified with him (Luke 23.40–3).

11. J. A. Findlay, *Jesus, Divine and Human*, Epworth Press 1938, pp. 67–9.

12. E.g. Thielicke, *Theological Ethics*, Robinson, *Groundwork of Christian Ethics*.

13. Jesus carried out non-emergency healings on the Sabbath day (Luke 13.10–17), and was accused of blasphemy when he claimed to have authority to forgive sins (Mark 2.7). There was no clear distinction between moral, ceremonial and civil law. There is certainly no case of Jesus abrogating commandments which had a distinctly ethical thrust. See D. J. Moo, 'Jesus and the Authority of the Mosaic Law', *Journal for the Study of the New Testament*, 1984, pp. 3–49.

14. J. Moltmann, *The Crucified God*, SCM Press 1973, ch. 6. See also his *Religion, Revolution and the Future*, Scribner 1969, p. 68.

15. J. Moltmann, *The Future of Creation*, SCM Press 1977, p. 78.

16. Ibid., p. 79.

17. T. W. Manson, *The Servant Messiah*, Cambridge University Press 1961, pp. 72–3.

5 Punishment according to St Paul

1. Although not found guilty in a criminal court, Paul admits that he aided and abetted the murder of Stephen (Acts 22.20), 'When the saints were put to death I cast my vote against them' (Acts 26.10).

2. The Greek word translated 'expiation' has not necessarily anything to do with punishment. The use of the Greek word *hilasterion* is discussed at some length in *Dictionary of New Testament Theology*, ed. Colin Brown, vol. III, pp. 145ff., and by G. Kittel, *Theological Dictionary of the New Testament*, Eerdmans 1965, vol. III, pp. 318–23. It is used 22 times in the LXX and corresponds to the Hebrew word *kipper*. The idea conveyed is far removed from the crude pagan notion of propitiating a capricious and malevolent deity. G. F. Oehler is quoted as saying that 'the law nowhere indicates that in sacrifice an act of punishment is executed: it in no way asks us to look on the altar as a place of punishment.' G. von Rad concludes, 'Expiation was not a penalty but a saving event.' Although it has been the subject of much controversy among theologians, *hilasterion* is not something which *makes* God gracious. Rather it presupposes the grace of God.

3. Quoted by S. Cave, *The Doctrine of the Work of Christ*, Hodder and Stoughton 1937, p. 163.

4. F. W., Dillistone, *The Christian Understanding of Atonement*, Nisbet 1968, reissued SCM Press 1984, ch. 5.

5. D. P. Walker, *The Decline of Hell*, Routledge and Kegan Paul 1964, p. 207.

6. Ibid., ch. 7.

7. V. A. Demant, *The Theology of Society*, Faber and Faber 1947.

8. H. R. Mackintosh, *The Christian Experience of Forgiveness*, Collins 1961, p. 205.

9. Gustaf Aulen, *Christus Victor*, SPCK 1950, p. 83.

10. Manson, *Ethics and the Gospel*, p. 78.

11. F. Greeves, *The Meaning of Sin*, Epworth Press 1956, ch. 10.

12. John Oman, *Grace and Personality*, Cambridge University Press 1942, p. 126.

13. Peake's *Commentary*, p. 893.

14. See Thielicke, *Theological Ethics*, vol. I, ch. 6.

6 The Dilemma of Christian Ethics

1. Ramsey, op. cit., pp. 36–7.

2. Ibid.
3. Ibid.
4. Ibid.
5. C. E. B. Cranfield, 'Romans 1:18', *Scottish Journal of Theology* 21, 1968, pp. 330–5.
6. Walker, *Decline of Hell*, op. cit., pp. 101–2.
7. F. Stephen, *Liberty, Equality, Fraternity*, Cambridge University Press 1967, p. 315.
8. Walker, op. cit., p. 62.
9. Ibid., p. 39.
10. Ibid., pp. 37–8.
11. Ibid., p. 81.
12. E. Moberly, *Suffering: Innocent and Guilty*, ch. 7.
13. Quoted in J. H. Leckie, *The World to Come and Final Destiny*, T. & T. Clark 1922.
14. Quoted in E. Moberly, op. cit., ch. 7.
15. P. Watson, *The State as Servant of God*, SPCK 1946, p. 46.
16. Thielicke, op. cit., vol. II, ch. 7.
17. Watson, op. cit., p. 46.
18. Thielicke, op. cit., vol. II, ch. 7.
19. G. B. Caird, *Principalities and Powers*, Oxford University Press 1956, p. 29.

7   Criminal Responsibility

1. Joyce in *Beginning OT Study*, pp. 74–89.
2. J. Barton, in ibid., pp. 117–8, 151.
3. T. E. Jessop, *Law and Love*, SCM Press 1940, p. 57.
4. F. Tannenbaum, *Crime and the Community*, Columbia University Press 1951, ch. 2.
5. R. Oerton, *Who is the Criminal?*, Hodder and Stoughton 1968, pp. 17, 123.
6. William Temple, *Mens Creatrix*, Macmillan 1935, p. 225.
7. Ives, *History of Penal Methods*, p. 81.
8. R. Partridge, *Broadmoor*, Chatto and Windus 1953, p. 11.
9. C. Burt, *The Young Delinquent*, London University 1931, ch. 2.
10. Ibid.
11. J. Lange, *Crime is Destiny*, Allen and Unwin 1931.
12. W. A. Bonger, *An Introduction to Criminology*, Methuen 1936, pp. 28–9.
13. Ibid.
14. H. Rhodes, *The Criminals we Deserve*, Methuen 1937, p. 17.
15. Ibid., p. 123.
16. Tannenbaum, op. cit., p. 21.
17. A. E. Bottoms and R. H. Preston, *The Coming Penal Crisis*, Scottish Academic Press 1980.
18. L. Coser, *The Function of Social Conflicts*, Routledge and Kegan Paul 1956, ch. 7.
19. G. B. Shaw, *The Crime of Imprisonment*, Constable, n. d., p. 113.
20. Krafft-Ebing, *Psychopathia Sexualis*, Staples Press 1965.
21. R. B. Cattell, *Crooked Personalities in Childhood and After*, Nisbet 1938, p. 150.
22. Sir Gervais Rentoul, *Sometimes I Think*, Hodder and Stoughton 1940, ch. 18.
23. Grace Pailthorpe, *Studies in the Psychology of Delinquency*, HMSO 1932, pp. 28–9.
24. Ethel Mannin, *Commonsense and the Child*, Jarrold 1931.
25. A. Bjerre, *The Psychology of Murder*, Longmans Green 1927, pp. 78–119.
26. Bonger, op. cit., p. 55.
27. E. Moberly, op. cit., ch. 9.

8   The Purpose of Punishment

1. W. Moberly, *Ethics of Punishment*, p. 186.
2. Ibid., p. 198.
3. Ibid., p. 187.
4. Ibid., p. 190.
5. Ibid., p. 197.
6. A. C. Ewing, *The Morality of Punishment*, Kegan Paul 1929, p. 35.

7. Kant in Ewing, op. cit., p. 15.
8. W. Moberly, op cit., p. 82.
9. T. H. Green quoted in ibid., p. 83.
10. Ewing, op. cit., p. 29.
11. Ibid., p. 26.
12. Ives, op. cit., ch. 4.
13. M. Wilson, *The Crime of Punishment*, Jonathan Cape 1931, ch. 4.
14. N. L. Robinson, *Christian Justice*, Swarthmore 1922, p. 176.
15. John Howard, *The State of Prisons in England and Wales*, William Eyres 1777.
16. A. Griffiths, *Memorials of Millbank*, Henry King 1875.
17. L. W. Fox, *The Modern English Prison*, Routledge 1934.
18. R. and H. Hauser, *The Fraternal Society*, Bodley Head 1962, pp. 50–60.
19. G. Sykes, *The Society of Captives*, Princeton University Press 1958, pp. 50–60.
20. William Temple, *The Ethics of Penal Action*, Clark Hall 1934.
21. H. Mannheim, *The Dilemma of Penal Reform*, Allen and Unwin 1939, p. 27.
22. Ibid., pp. 53–81.
23. G. B. Shaw, Preface to S. and B. Webb, *English Prisons under Local Government*, Charles Scribners 1922, p. xiv.
24. Wilson, op. cit., ch. 6.
25. K. Menninger, *The Crime of Punishment*, Viking 1969, p. 280.
26. Bottoms and Preston, op. cit.

9 *The Relevance of an Ideal*

1. C. J. Cadoux, *The Early Christian Attitude to War*, Allen and Unwin 1940, pp. 156–7.
2. F. J. Foakes-Jackson, *The History of the Christian Church*, Allen and Unwin 1914, p. 284.
3. Ives, op. cit., ch. 1.
4. See W. Robinson, *Christianity is Pacifism*, Allen and Unwin 1933, p. 114.
5. Ives, op. cit., pp. 40–1.
6. Ibid., pp. 42–3.
7. *British Encyclopaedia*, vol. VI, p. 155.
8. Ives, op. cit., pp. 58–76.
9. G. Rupp, *Martin Luther*, Lutterworth 1945, p. 94.
10. Watson, *The State as Servant of God*, op. cit., p. 46.
11. W. Andrews, *Bygone Punishments*, W. Andrews 1899.
12. Thielicke, op. cit., vol. II, part 5.
13. Sir Norman Anderson in *Law, Morality and the Bible*, ed. B. N. Kaye and G. J. Wenham, Inter-Varsity Press 1978, pp. 230–49.
14. John Wesley, *Letters*, Epworth Press 1931, vol. VIII, p. 145; see also *Journal*, Epworth Press 1938, vol. VII, p. 295.
15. L. Orman Cooper, *John Howard*, p. 135.
16. C. G. Oakes, *Sir Samuel Romilly*, Allen and Unwin 1935.
17. Wilson op. cit., ch. 1.
18. W. Moberly, op. cit., pp. 32–4.
19. Griffiths, op. cit.
20. Free Church Council, *Penal Reform*, 1964, p. 9.
21. Reinhold Niebuhr, *An Interpretation of Christian Ethics*, SCM Press 1960.

Index of Biblical References